NETWORKING
LIKE A PRO®

TURNING CONTACTS INTO CONNECTIONS

Ivan Misner, PhD
David Alexander & Brian Hilliard

E
Entrepreneur
Press

Jere L. Calmes, Publisher
Cover Design: Desktop Miracles
Composition and Production: Eliot House Productions

This publication is designed to provide accurate and authoritative information
in regard to the subject matter covered. It is sold with the understanding that the
publisher is not engaged in rendering legal, accounting, or other professional
services. If legal advice or other expert assistance is required, the services of a
competent professional person should be sought.

> —From a Declaration of Principles jointly adopted by a
> Committee of the American Bar Association and
> a Committee of Publishers and Associations

Givers Gain® and VCP Process® are registered trademarks of BNI.
Certified Networker® and Referrals for Life® are registered trademarks of the
Referral Institute.
Networking Like a Pro!® is a registered trademark of Agito Consulting.

Library of Congress Cataloging-in-Publication
Misner, Ivan R., 1956–
    Networking like a pro/by Ivan Misner, David Alexander, Brian Hilliard.
    p. cm.
     ISBN-13: 978-1-59918-356-5 (alk. paper)
     ISBN-10: 1-59918-356-0 (alk. paper)
     1. Business networks. 2. Business referrals. I. Alexander, David G. II.
Hilliard, Brian. III. Title.
HD69.S8M5724 2009
650.1'3—dc22   2009010903

Printed in Canada

13 12 11 10 09   10 9 8 7 6 5 4 3 2

Contents

PART II. YOUR NETWORKING STRATEGY

PART III. NETWORKING FACE TO FACE

Acknowledgments

The three of us went into writing *Networking Like a Pro* fully understanding that co-authoring a book takes even more commitment, dedication, and effort than going it alone since co-authors have to blend ideas with one another in a way that moves the book forward and creates cohesion throughout the entire text. Sometimes though, accomplishing that does not come easily, to say the least—especially when there are deadlines to be held accountable to.

With that said, we have each marveled on numerous occasions at how immediately and naturally our individual contributions to this book intertwined and how, as a result, the entire process of co-authoring this book together was not only relatively stress-free, but also consistently enjoyable to dedicate time and effort to. We are each very grateful for the unique experience and insight each one of us brought to the table and for the opportunity to collaborate on writing this book together.

However, our cumulative efforts would not have come together nearly as successfully if it weren't for our highly knowledgeable editing team: Jeff Morris, Karen Billipp, and Elizabeth Tripp. An editor's job can unfortunately be a thankless one and we would like to state, for the record, that this book would not be what it is today without the energy and talents of our three editors—you all did an amazing job.

We would also like to acknowledge our publisher, Entrepreneur Press. They are a company which has proven to be a class-act operation through and through and it's no wonder Ivan has done three other books with them.

Finally, we saved the best for last as we owe the biggest thanks to our families who have supported us over the entire course of creating this book. Thank you to the Misner, Alexander, and Hilliard families for your love, patience, and encouragement. We hope we make you proud.

Myths, Mysteries, and Misconceptions

magine being dropped off in a foreign city with nothing but a few hundred dollars and being told that the only way to get home is to start a business and make a lot of money—in six days. Well, you don't have to imagine it. Just watch the BBC television show *The Last Millionaire*.

In this "reality" show inspired by Donald Trump's *Apprentice* on American television, 12 of the United Kingdom's most successful young entrepreneurs pair off in a series of competitions. They are taken to cities around the world where—without their accustomed luxury, without the aid of their companies, colleagues, or friends, without access to their bank accounts, often without even knowing the local language, culture, or customs—the pairs are told to build a business from scratch. The team that makes the most money in a week gets to go home; the rest go on to compete in another city. After the last two teams face off, the last surviving pair are pitted against each other to win the honor of not being the last millionaire.

On one episode, the final contenders, Natalie and Lucy, were flown to Hong Kong and lodged in a cheap hostel. They were each given the equivalent of a few hundred U.S. dollars and told to create a product and sell it in five days. They could recruit student helpers from a list they were both given, but otherwise they were left pretty much on their own.

Natalie called the student contacts for help. Lucy, however, went to an internet café, pulled up Google, and typed *business networking* into the search engine. The first hit was BNI, the world's largest business networking organization. Lucy called the president of one of Hong Kong's chapters and wrangled an invitation to visit the group's next meeting.

Minutes after giving the group a 30-second presentation on her business goals, she was networking with members and getting referrals for contacts that would design, produce, and sell her product—T-shirts. Among these referrals were the largest manufacturing agent in Asia and one of the top manufacturers in Hong Kong. A couple of days later, her new business was off to the races.

Want to know who won? Lucy, of course. Her earnings were 16 times her startup money and more than 4 times what Natalie made.

Think of it: in a time when businesses worldwide are struggling, an ambitious person with good business sense can be dropped into a foreign city and—with a little help from some business networkers—build a profitable business in less than a week. To people who are not familiar with the power of networking, that is astounding! There's not a more vivid testament to the power of referral networking—at least, not on television.

Networkers know. As the three of us cross continents and oceans, giving presentations and conducting seminars to spread the word about the power of relationship networking, we are greeted by audiences of enthusiastic businesspeople eager to supercharge their enterprises by becoming networking professionals. But at the same time, and in the same settings, we are often bombarded with questions that reveal how much myth and misinformation exists about networking as a marketing tool: Is referral networking truly effective, or is it just a way to pick up the occasional new client? Can it be considered a legitimate business strategy? Aren't direct mail, billboards, even Yellow Pages ads more important?

The truth is that referral networking is becoming an accepted and important marketing strategy in businesses worldwide. Obviously, there's a very good reason for this: it works. It's a cost-effective way to get in front of a bunch of new clients, and it's a much better way to keep a business prospering over the long term, because it's built on mutually beneficial relationships between you and your fellow business owners. It's powered by the oldest and most enduring principle of human society: Givers Gain,® the idea that the good you do will eventually come back to you in one form or another.

DEBUNKING THE BUNK

As business professionals, we can tell you from personal experience how effective referral networking has been in the success of our own businesses. After reading this book, you will understand how it works and how it can be effective in your own business. But let's start by addressing some of the myths and misconceptions that people hit us with from time to time.

"I tried networking. It didn't work.
What's different about this?"

It's a common misconception that simply attending a networking event will bring you new business right away. It won't. Neither will just reading this book; there's no silver bullet in these pages.

Networking is simple, but it's not easy. If it were easy, everyone would do it, and do it well. But not everyone does. That's because it's a skill, like cooking and golf and carpentry, that takes knowledge, practice, commitment, and effort to learn and apply consistently. You can't just go out to the golf course, buy a club and a ball, whack the ball around a bit, and think you've played a round of golf. Neither can you walk unprepared into a gathering of potential networking contacts and suddenly become a competent networker—no matter how gregarious and sociable you are or how many books on networking you've read.

Networking is about forming and nurturing mutually beneficial relationships, which brings you new connections with large numbers of people, some of whom will become good customers. Networking also puts you in touch with other resources, such as industry experts, accountants, and lawyers, who can help your business in other ways.

Over time, you will get new business and your operation will grow stronger and more profitable. Will it happen overnight? No, and your new customers probably won't be among the first 10 or even 100 people you talk to, either. New business will come from people your networking contacts refer to you. But first you have to form solid relationships with your fellow networkers.

Some people go to a chamber of commerce mixer, exchange a few business cards, then say, "There. I've networked." Wrong. That's only the beginning. You have to attend a variety of events to broaden your networking base; follow up with new contacts and learn all you can about their businesses, their goals, and their lives; maintain close ties with established contacts; provide referrals, information, and other benefits to your fellow networkers; and generally cultivate these relationships and keep them strong and healthy. That's networking. Only after you've been at it for quite some time will you begin to see a return on your investment. But when it comes, the return is strong and durable.

"Aren't most networking groups just people like me who are trying to build up a new business?"

When you go to a presentation or a seminar on networking, you might get that impression, because the people you meet are there to learn something new, and so they tend to be younger folks. But if you go to a regular networking event or join a networking organization, you'll soon see that many of the people there tend to be older, established businesspeople. In fact, in the typical business networking group, the members range in age from the 20s through the 60s, and based on a study done at St. Thomas University, two-thirds of them are over 40. There's a good reason for this. It's usually the seasoned pros who have long since recognized and learned to use the benefits of networking to bolster their business. Many have used networking throughout the life of their business and are fully aware of the competitive advantage it offers. Older networkers often serve as mentors for younger businesspeople, which can be an enormous advantage to someone who is new to the art and science of networking.

The best networking groups are the ones whose membership is diverse in many ways. That is they have not only older and younger members but also a good balance of men and women, a mixture of races and ethnicities that is representative of the community, and a wide variety of professions and specialties. Such a group offers the best opportunities to get referrals from outside your immediate circle of acquaintances and experience, which puts you on the fast track to expanding your business.

"What good is networking if you can't measure the results?"

If you're expecting to find a direct, immediate correlation between your networking activities and the dollars you harvest as a result, you're going to be sorely disappointed. It's not like cold calling, where you can check off 500 phone numbers and see that you talked to 50 people and closed 7 sales and that 493 of your calls were a huge waste of your time. It's not like sending out 1,000 mailers and getting just 3 of them back, which gives you a hard number (exactly 0.3 percent) but pretty wimpy results (exactly 0.3 percent). If your goal is immediate results, no matter how poor, these alternatives may be right up your alley. Mass advertising? Sure, it works, but even that traditional method can't tell you exactly how many customers came into your store as a result of the enormous sum of money you spent.

The returns you receive through networking are like the apples you pick from an orchard you started from a single seed. You don't expect anything the first year, or even the second or third. But in the fourth year that tree will not only bear fruit but also spread the seeds that will ultimately become a whole grove of apple trees. With networking, the time scale is not that daunting; it may not take years to start seeing results, but it will probably take many months. You might get a few early referrals, but the real payoff in measurable business comes after you've stuck with it long enough to build a substantial referral network. That's when you'll find that you're getting referrals from people you never knew about, people who are connected to you only through several intermediaries, so many and from so many sources that you may not even know exactly how many are the result of your networking.

Although the full complexity of your network may not be apparent even to you, the results of a good referral networking system are measurable. Toward the end of this book, in Chapter

29 and in Appendix II, you'll find our Networking Scorecard, a tool for keeping track of your networking efforts. No, this is not a direct measure of the sales you're getting, but as you become an experienced businessperson, you'll find that the information on networking says volumes about the condition of your network and its implications in terms of your eventual sales and business volume.

Here's another way to measure your networking success: of the people you meet at a networking event, what percentage of them remember you 72 hours later? This is one measure of your *visible identity,* and it's only one factor, but a significant one, in determining how successfully you are networking. Networking is more than just meeting people, and it isn't about how many sales you get from the people you meet. It's about how well you are remembered by a new contact and whether you differentiated yourself from the other five people she met that day.

One of the most important metrics is the number of *coffee connections* (follow-up meetings) you have with your new contacts—at least, the ones you want to network with. A contact that you do not follow up with is a contact that will never become part of your network. There will be no business—no sales, no referrals, no meeting the powerful CEO he knows—unless you follow through.

You can measure the results, but you have to be tracking the right networking activities. Most big companies have their salespeople track the wrong activities, and they can't understand why their networking efforts are not working. To get the results you expect, you've got to track the right efforts.

"If my customers are satisfied, they'll give me referrals. Why should I join a networking group?"

Yes, customers can be a good source of referrals. Immediately after an especially good experience at your business, a happy client may talk you up to a friend who needs the service you provide. But it often ends there. A customer who is merely satisfied is not likely to go out of her way to tell others about you. And here's the kicker: A customer who is unhappy with you will tell a lot of people—11 times as many as a happy customer, by one study. Customer-based word-of-mouth can hurt you more than help you.

A networking partner, by contrast, is always on the lookout for good customers for your business, just as you are always looking for people to send to your networking partners. Your fellow networkers also know more about your business and the kind of customers you want, and they are experts in marketing you by word of mouth, the most powerful kind of marketing that exists. This kind of referral generation lasts much longer and brings you a steady stream of high-quality business, the kind that doesn't turn around and go to your competitor as soon as he holds his next clearance sale. You can get more good referrals from one or two loyal networking sources than from all the customers who come through your doors—and the customers you'll get are the kind you'll want to keep.

"How do I network if I'm not a naturally outgoing person?"

Go ahead and breathe a sigh of relief, because you don't have to become Mr. Public Speaker, person-about-town, to be a successful networker. Most businesspeople, given a little real-world experience, naturally develop a certain level of comfort in dealing with customers, vendors, and others in their day-to-day transactions. Even people who are not gregarious or outgoing can form meaningful relationships and communicate.

Over years of teaching people the art of networking, we've found many techniques that can make the process a whole lot easier—especially for those who consider themselves a bit introverted. For example, volunteering to be an ambassador or visitor host for a local business networking event can be a great way to get involved without feeling out of place.

IVAN

Recently my wife and I were sitting at the table having dinner and talking when I made an offhand comment about being an extrovert. She gave me a look and said, "Honey, I hate to break it to you, but you're an introvert."

I smiled and said, "Yeah, right. I'm a public speaker, and I'm the founder of the world's largest networking organization. And you say I'm an introvert?"

She then proceeded to name all the ways in which I was an introvert, supporting her argument with real-life examples of my behavior. I still couldn't believe it. But we've been married for 20 years, and I had a sneaking suspicion she might actually know me pretty well.

The next day I did some research on the internet and found a test I could take. The results were a shock: I was a "situational extrovert"! That meant I was somewhat of a loner, reserved around strangers, but very outgoing in the right context.

That's when it finally hit me. "Oh my god! I'm an introvert!"

When I visit a BNI region, I ask the director to have someone walk me around and introduce me to members and visitors, so I can connect with as many people as possible, I tell her—but in reality, it's because I'm uncomfortable walking around alone and introducing myself. Oh my god, I'm an introvert!

I realized that the whole notion of acting like the host, not the guest and volunteering to be the ambassador at a chamber event or the visitor host at a BNI group were not just activities I recommended to all those poor introverts out there, they were all ways that I, myself, employed to move around more comfortably at networking events. Oh my god, I'm an introvert! Who would have thought? (Besides my lovely wife, that is.)

Now, more than ever, I truly believe that whether you are an introvert or an extrovert, you can be good at networking. There are strengths and weaknesses to both traits; by finding ways to enhance the strengths and minimize the weaknesses, anyone can be a great networker.

BRIAN

This one really hits home for me. If you've seen me on stage talking to a bunch of folks and having a good time, you might find it hard to believe that I'm not a naturally outgoing person. But it's the truth. As someone who talks about sales and networking, I had to learn these techniques to help me get more business.

I knew early on that if I wanted to build my business through referrals, I would need to get better at meeting new people. So I picked up a few books, jotted down some thoughts—and here I am.

Think about it. When you have guests at your house or office, what do you do? You engage them, make them feel comfortable, perhaps offer them something to drink. What you don't do is stand by yourself in the corner thinking about how you hate meeting new people.

By serving as a visitor host at your local chamber event, you effectively become the host of the party. Try it! You'll find it much easier to meet and talk to new people.

> **"Getting business by person-to-person referral sounds like something that used to happen when my great-grandfather was selling horse-drawn buggies. Why should I waste my time on a marketing method that's generations out of date?"**

Yes, networking has been around a long time. It used to be the way that most businesses operated. In a small community, where everybody knows everybody, people do business with the people they trust, and they recommend these businesses to their friends. Small-town professionals naturally tend to refer business to each other, too, usually to those who return the favor, but often simply on the basis of whose service will reflect best on the referrer. If you're a plumber and you refer a customer to a dentist you know, you don't want that customer complaining to you a week later about what a lousy dentist you sent him to.

Today, most people do business on a larger scale, over a broader customer base and geographic area. More people now live in cities, and in even a small city most people are total strangers to one another. The personal connections of the old-style community, and the trust that went with them, are mostly gone. That's why a system for generating referrals among a group of professionals who trust one another is so important these days, and it is why referral networking is not only the way of the past but the wave of the future. It's a cost-effective strategy with a long-term payoff.

It's where business marketing is going, and it's where you need to go if you're going to stay in the game. As the great hockey player Wayne Gretzky said, "I don't skate to where the puck is, but where it's going to be."

"Networking is not a hard science."

IVAN

I once suggested to the business dean of a large university that the business curriculum should include courses in networking. His response? "My professors would never teach that material here. It's all soft science."

I should not have been surprised, because I've run into this attitude many times at many business schools. But it shocked me to hear it at a progressive major university.

We give people bachelor's degrees in marketing, business, and even entrepreneurship, but we teach them hardly anything about the one subject that virtually every entrepreneur says is critically important to his business: networking and social capital. Why don't business schools teach this subject? I think it's because most are made up of professors who've never owned a business. They've learned almost everything they know about running a business from books and consulting.

Can you imagine a law course taught by someone who was not an attorney or an accounting course taught by anyone without direct accounting experience? Yet we put business professors in colleges to teach marketing and entrepreneurship with little or no firsthand experience in the field. Is it any wonder, then, that a subject so critically important to business people is so completely missed by business schools?

The science of networking is finally being codified and structured. Business schools around the world need to wake up and start teaching this curriculum. Schools with vision, foresight, and the ability to act swiftly (the way business professors say businesses should act) will be positioning themselves as leaders in education by truly understanding and responding to the needs of today's businesses.

At the end of our conversation, I asked the dean, "How are courses on leadership any less a soft science than networking?" He didn't have an answer.

The school has since replaced this dean with a new one who believes that emotional intelligence is an important thing to teach our college students. There may be hope yet!

WAVE OF THE FUTURE

Think about the most successful people you know. What do they have in common? Probably this: They have built a network of contacts that provide support, information, and business referrals. They have mastered the art and science of networking, and business flows their way almost as a matter of course.

It has taken these successful networkers years of hard work and perseverance to build their networks. It will take a similar commitment from you, too, but it won't take you as long, because you'll have one great advantage over the others: you'll have this book.

In these pages we will show you how to develop and use a referral network as a long-term, sustainable business client-acquisition strategy, employing the tactics that have been found most effective by the pros. You will learn of many tools and techniques that will make it easier for you to build profitable relationships. You'll learn them faster than those who have gone before you and had to learn them by trial and error. Using this marketing strategy, you will be able to maintain a high profit margin while providing better service to your clients, a combination that will put you far ahead of your competition.

Networking is the mainstream business development technique of the future. Businesspeople who invest in themselves by learning how to network like a pro will be rewarded with a long-term sustainable and profitable business.

PART I

THE NETWORKING MIND-SET

1

Social Capital

You've heard of financial capital, but do you know about social capital?

Financial capital is the material wealth, whether money or property, that is accumulated by individuals and businesses and used, or available for use, in the production of more wealth. This is the standard definition in economics.

Social capital is the accumulation of resources developed in the course of social interactions, especially through personal and professional networks. These resources include ideas, knowledge, information, opportunities, contacts, and, of course, referrals.

They also include trust, confidence, friendship, good deeds, and goodwill.

Like financial capital, social capital is accumulated by individuals and businesses and used in the production of wealth. Unlike financial capital, social capital is intangible, but it's every bit as real as financial capital. Although it is difficult or impossible to measure precisely, it can be even more powerful than financial capital in terms of eventual return on investment.

Social capital is built by design, not by chance. According to Wayne Baker, author of *Achieving Success Through Social Capital*:

> *Studies show that lucky people increase their chances of being in the right place at the right time by building a "spider web structure" of relationships that catch information. . . . Success is social: all the ingredients of success that we customarily think of as individual—talent, intelligence, education, effort, and luck—are intertwined with networks.*

Thus, a key way that social capital is acquired is through the process of networking. Successful networking is all about building and maintaining solid professional relationships. The trouble is that we don't live in *Little House on the Prairie* anymore and we no longer have these natural community-like business relationships. Many people hardly know their own neighbors, let alone the business people who run the shops and stores down at the local strip mall. Yet, more than ever, networking is critical for an individual's success in business.

BACK TO THE FUTURE

Networking is the kind of social and professional interaction that came naturally to business people throughout most of this nation's history, especially in smaller communities. But as villages grew into towns, and towns into cities, and cities into megalopolises, the sense of community, and the close, personal business relationships that went with it, gradually disappeared. The rise of large retail chains and multinational corporations, along with the demise of small businesses under the stiff price competition from these giants, further weakened the natural networking that existed.

The disappearance of community-based networking has left a vacuum that is now being filled by strong-contact networks. Business networking organizations such as BNI create a virtual main street for business professionals—an environment and a system for passing referrals that is the 21st-century equivalent of the traditional model for doing business.

As Eric Lesser, in his book *Knowledge and Social Capital*, notes, "Without a shared understanding of common terms, activities, and outcomes, it becomes very difficult to reap the benefits associated with building social capital." The power of business networking organizations is that they provide these common terms, activities, and outcomes in a system that is designed specifically to accomplish this goal.

When you join and attend meetings in a business networking group, you build social capital in a number of ways. You gain the trust and friendship of fellow members; you provide valuable referrals; you contribute knowledge and skills to the effort; you become more knowledgeable and improve your social and business skills. Not least, you get out of your cave—the self-imposed isolation that many business people fall prey to.

Like financial capital, social capital not only is earned and accumulated but can also be spent. This is the idea underlying BNI's guiding principle, Givers Gain®: the good you do comes back to you, over the long term and often in indirect ways. You accumulate social capital by providing help, advice, information, referrals, and other benefits to your fellow networkers with no thought of a quid pro quo. By gaining the trust of others, gratitude for value provided, and a solid reputation for integrity and expertise, you become a person whom others wish to help whenever an opportunity to do so presents itself.

DAVID

A financial advisor I worked with for several years started a chapter of BNI and became very active as its president. He gave more referrals than anyone else in the chapter; however, he got very few back.

He came to me a little frustrated about this. I told him it takes time to build trust, especially in his industry. I recommended several books on the subject and suggested he attend some training programs I was offering. His response surprised me. He said, "Train me to train the programs."

I said, "Aren't you concerned that you're already giving a lot more than you're getting?"

He said, "Yes, but I know that trust takes time, and giving people valuable training at my expense will build trust."

He became my lead trainer and assistant director in Winston-Salem, North Carolina, and continued to give even more of his time and energy. His network rewarded him in an amazing way. Over the next 24 months, he received referrals worth $36 million—proving once more that givers always gain in the end.

OUTSIDE THE CAVE

Social capital works for everybody, not just people who set out purposefully to become networkers. A colleague of ours works in a profession that entails a minimal amount of day-to-day interaction with others: writing and editing. He handles a limited number of projects, usually no more than two or three books at a time, and works long hours and days in isolation, surfacing occasionally to communicate with an author or publisher about details. You might say he works in a cave with only a few airholes.

How does a cave dweller build social capital? This particular editor, feeling the isolation, crawled out of his cave one day and went looking for company. He joined a small band of writers who were forming a professional organization. Energized, he joined their efforts to build the organization, attract new members, publish a newsletter, schedule presentations and speakers, arrange conferences with editors and agents, and even throw a few parties to lure other writers out of their caves. All of this work was done by volunteers who got a kick out of building a service organization that would help writers network with one another and achieve success.

The organization grew and became the largest networking organization for writers in the nation. While this was happening, our friend the editor made several new friends among the organization's founding members. One of them told him of a job opening that turned into a 12-year-long salaried position; this gave him the steady income he needed to support his family. Another friend, a low-volume publisher of high-quality books, gave him several editing projects and, after his salaried job ended, a full schedule of freelance work.

Many of the authors this publisher referred to the editor returned again and again with other projects for other publishers. One of these writers was Dr. Ivan Misner, co-author of this book and more than a dozen others, on most of which he has worked with the same cave-dwelling editor.

Although the editor didn't know it when he began this low-key form of networking, he was building social capital when he thought he was only having fun. Over the years, the interest on this social capital began flowing back to him in many different forms, with no direct connection to the benefits he had helped provide to other writers.

RELATIONSHIPS ARE CURRENCY

How many times have you seen an entrepreneur (maybe even yourself) go to a networking event, meet a bunch of good people, then leave and never talk to them again? Too often, right? And it's not because he doesn't like them or ever want to see them again but because he's a busy, busy person with so much going on that he can't even remember what he had for breakfast, let alone reconnect with individuals he just met.

It's a shame, because such new contacts are where future business is born.

Don't be misled: it's not the number of contacts you make that's important; it's the ones you turn into lasting relationships. There's quite a difference. Try making ten cold calls and introducing yourself. OK, how well did that go?

Now call five people you already know and tell them you're putting together a marketing plan for the coming year and you would appreciate any help they could provide, in the form of either a referral or new business.

Better results behind door #2, right? Of course. You already have a relationship with these folks, and depending on how deep it is, most of them would be glad to help you.

So here's the question: How can you deepen the relationships with people you already know to the point where they might be willing to help you out in the future? Here are four quick steps to get you moving in the right direction.

1. *Give your clients a personal call.* Find out how things went with the project you were involved in. Ask if there's anything else you can do to help. Important: do not ask for a referral at this point.
2. *Make personal calls to all the people who have helped you or referred business to you.* Ask them how things are going. Try to learn more about their current activities so you can refer business to them.
3. *Put together a hit list of 50 people you'd like to stay in touch with this year.* Include anyone who has given you business in the last 12 months (from steps 1 and 2) as well as any other prospects you've connected with recently. Send them cards on the next holiday (Memorial Day, Independence Day, Labor Day, etc.).
4. *Two weeks after you've sent them cards, call them and see what's going on.* If they're past clients or people you've talked to before, now is the perfect time to ask for a referral. If they're prospects, perhaps you can set up an appointment to have coffee and find out if their plans might include using your services.

See how easy that was? After a few weeks, you'll have more than enough social capital to tap into the rest of the year.

Social capital is the international currency of networking, especially business networking. If you take as much care in raising and investing your social capital as you do your financial capital, you'll find that the benefits that flow from these intangible investments not only will be rewarding in themselves but also will multiply your material returns many times over.

2

The Law of Reciprocity

The term *reciprocity* is at the center of relationship networking, but it is often misunderstood. *Webster's* dictionary defines reciprocity as "a mutual or cooperative interchange of favors or privileges," as when actions taken for the benefit of others are returned in kind. This leads many inexperienced networkers to expect an immediate return for any actions they take on behalf of another. Givers gain, right?

Wrong. Think of it this way: The first word in Givers Gain® is *givers*. This is important. It signifies that the act of giving is the first and most important part of the principle. It does not, however, mean that every act of giving will be immediately rewarded by the recipient. On the contrary, the idea driving Givers Gain is, paradoxically, the principle of giving without the expectation of an immediate return.

IT'S THE LAW

In networking, this idea is called the *law of reciprocity*. The law of reciprocity differs from the standard notion of reciprocity in that the giver cannot, should not, and does not expect an immediate return on her investment in another person's gain. The only thing that she can be sure of is that, given enough effort and time, her generosity will be returned by and through her network of contacts, associates, friends, family, colleagues, and others—many times over and in many different ways.

The law of reciprocity validates the abundance mindset by proving that there is far more business to be gained by referring business to others than you might at first expect. If you go into relationship networking thinking that simply giving a referral is enough to get you a referral in return, you're confusing a relationship with a transaction. As pointed out in *Truth or Delusion*, by Dr. Ivan Misner, Mike Macedonio, and Mike Garrison, the law of reciprocity is not simply a quid pro quo; it's providing benefits (including referrals) to others in order to create strong networking relationships that will eventually bring benefits (especially referrals) to you, often in a very roundabout way rather than directly from the person you benefit. This makes the law of reciprocity an enormously powerful tool for growing your own business' size and profitability.

Here are some things to keep in mind as you learn to use the law of reciprocity:

- *Giving means helping others achieve success.* What is your plan to contribute to others? How much time and energy can you

DAVID

Many years ago, I sold telecommunications services in North Carolina. One of my best connections was with a data communications company—a match seemingly made in referral heaven. Yet it did not produce results for me until I unintentionally used the law of reciprocity. One day, in an impulsive rush of generosity, I said to the owner, "If you ever get into a bind and need an extra hand, give me a call."

I never expected him to take me up on it—had, in fact, forgotten about it—until one night I got a call from him. Would I please come out and help with a network installation? He was shorthanded and up against a deadline.

I headed out to help and wound up pulling cables through a building all night. I went home exhausted but with his heartfelt thanks, a little pocket money—and nothing else. Nevertheless, I felt pleased that I had been able to help.

Less than a month later, he sent me one of the biggest referrals of my career, which resulted in a $50,000 contract with another company. He continued to be a rich source of referrals, too. The law of reciprocity had proved its worth to me.

spare for this? Do you actively seek out opportunities to help people? You could volunteer to help out with something that's important to someone in your network, offer advice or support in time of need, or even work hard to connect someone to a valuable contact of yours.

- *The person who helps you will not necessarily be the person you helped.* Zig Ziglar says, "If you help enough people get what they want, you will get what you want." In other words, what goes around comes around. If you focus intently on helping others, you will achieve success in the end.
- *The law of reciprocity can be measured.* This is our answer to the myth (see Introduction) that networking cannot be measured: we use the Networking Scorecard, part of the Certified Networker Program® that's offered through the Referral Institute. To see how it works, try using the simplified version in Figure 2.1 for a few weeks. If you're applying the law of reciprocity consistently, you will see your weekly total score gradually rise.

Figure 2.1
Networking Scorecard Worksheet

Week of:							
Action	**Points**	**Mon**	**Tue**	**Wed**	**Thur**	**Fri**	**Total**
Send a thank-you card	1×						
Send a gift	1×						
Referral (level = points; 10 levels)							
Send an article of interest	5×						
Arrange a group activity for clients	50×						
Nominate someone	10×						
Include others in newsletter	5×						
Arrange a speaking engagement	10×						
Total							

- *Success takes getting involved.* Contrary to Woody Allen's assertion that "90 percent of success is just showing up," you have to do more than simply be present to be a successful networker. If you join a chamber of commerce, become an ambassador. If you join a BNI chapter, get involved in the leadership team. If you join a civic organization, get on a committee. The law of reciprocity requires giving to the group; it will pay you back many times over.

THE ABUNDANCE MIND-SET

As a businessperson who is just starting to network, you might find yourself in a crisis of confidence in the first few months. You've been attending events, meeting new contacts, collecting business cards, forming new relationships, handing out referrals right and left, helping other businesspeople solve problems, but receiving no referrals in return. You've been assured that seeing no immediate return is nothing unusual, but you are getting discouraged because you've put out all that effort on behalf of other businesses and gained no new clients. You're getting a nagging feeling that it's a sucker's game, that despite your generous efforts nobody else cares what happens to you; you may even feel you've lost ground by neglecting your own business.

So when an experienced networker then tells you to give some business to someone whose business is similar to yours, whose market overlaps your own, your reaction is sheer panic. Give business to a competitor? In what universe?

Businesspeople sometimes feel that there's a strictly limited amount of business to be had and that their job is to corral as much of it as possible at the expense of their competitors. But the fact is that the amount of business, in most cases, far exceeds the available vendor capacity. Scarcity is an illusion.

No two vendors offer exactly the same lineup of products or services to their clients. You and your competitors have different preferences about what kinds of business you provide and what kinds of clients you serve. If you explore the possibilities, you will often find that your interests dovetail with those of a competitor, either in your offerings or your geographic service area. By referring your less desirable business to a competitor who prefers it, you can position yourself to receive the competitor's surplus business, the kind you want to get, in return.

Understanding and using this coincidence of interests with your competitors is part of what networkers call an abundance mind-set. It is part of the principle of Givers Gain, and it operates

IVAN

When I was building my first consulting business, I became involved with a large project that required more than one consultant in my field of business consulting. As a result, I found myself teamed up with a competitor, an arrangement that turned out to be of mutual benefit to us both. My competitor preferred doing budgeting and financial consulting work for our clients, so I handed over that work to him; in return, he sent human resources and strategic planning jobs to me, which pleased me mightily.

After the project was completed, my competitor and I decided we liked the arrangement so much that we kept referring business to each other along the same lines. In fact, we got other professionals involved and formed a power team, a group of businesses that were related to ours but not competing with us and to which it was natural to refer business.

according to the law of reciprocity. By giving business to others—in this case, your competitors—you will be rewarded down the line, quite possibly in ways you didn't anticipate or from a source you weren't aware of. There's more than enough business to go around, and this is the principle that underlies the abundance mind-set.

A master networker understands that, although networking is not the end but simply the means to growing a business, service to your network of contacts must always be uppermost in your networking activities. Once you have established a solid reputation as someone who cares about the success of others, the law of reciprocity will reward you with an abundance of high-quality referrals.

3

Farming for Referrals

I f we could impart one piece of wisdom regarding networking and getting more referrals, it would be this: networking is about farming for new contacts, not hunting them. It's a point that needs to be made, because most business professionals go about networking the way our cave-dwelling ancestors did when hunting for food—aggressively and carrying a big stick.

You'll see them at any gathering of businesspeople. They're so busy looking for the next big sale or trying to meet the "right" prospect that they approach networking simply as an exercise in sifting through crowds of people until they bag the ideal client, the big customer who can turn their business around. They don't have time for regular people like us; they're stalking the director of marketing, chief operating officer, or other high-octane connection, looking for the big kill.

"Farmers" take a different approach. They don't waste time looking for the right person; instead, like those who plant seeds and patiently nurture their crops, they seek to form and build relationships wherever they can find them. If they get an immediate payoff, that's fine, but it's not their principal goal. They know that the effort expended upfront will pay off in a rich harvest later on—much richer than the hunter's quick kill—and that truly profitable relationships can't be rushed.

DROP THE GUN, GRAB THE PLOW

As a business professional seeking to get more business through relationship networking, you need to know the difference between hunting and farming and act accordingly. It's easy to fall into the trap of hunting for the contact who's ready to buy your product or service right now, not six months down the road. We know you're tempted to be a hunter, because we're subject to the same pressures. You've got a lot going on and you need more business right away.

Although we understand the quest for fast money, there's just one problem: it's exactly the wrong approach. Relationship networking is about consistency and reliability: consistently meeting new people and reliably following up with the folks you have just met. It's about developing relationships with referral partners who can provide a steady stream of income far into the future—the opposite of fast money.

This is why thinking of networking as farming is so important. When you're meeting people for the first time, you should be planting the seeds for a lasting relationship. Instead of thinking about whether this person is ready to buy right now, you should focus on developing rapport. Here's how.

Ask the Right Questions

Don't ask qualifying questions, as if you're interviewing a new hire. Questions asked in a veiled attempt to determine whether the person is ready to do business rarely fool anyone; we call them see-through questions, because most prospects see right through them.

Instead, ask questions that demonstrate your genuine interest in the other person and her business:

DAVID

You'll notice that these questions—most of which focus on how the businessperson gets her clients and can therefore help you make referrals—elicit information that every person knows but is rarely asked about. We're more interested in people who seem interested in us. Call it a symptom of our me-centered culture, but I can't remember ever going to a networking event where people asked me how I built my business. If I were, I would be more inclined to keep in touch with that person and help him by sending him referrals. Farming, rather than hunting, for business gives you the flexibility to ask rapport-building questions, a big first step toward building a profitable referral partnership.

- How long have you been in the business?
- What made you want to start up this business? (assuming she's a business owner)
- What kind of clients do you typically work with?
- Where is your business located?
- What's your geographic coverage?

Offer Free Professional Advice

Let's say you're a real estate agent talking with someone at a networking event who, although not ready to buy a home today, is heading in that direction. You could say something like this:

> *Well, I know you're not interested in buying a home right now. But when you're ready to start looking, I'd highly recommend checking out the north part of town. A lot of my clients are seeing their homes appreciate in the 10 to 20 percent range, and from what I understand, the city is thinking about building another middle school in that area.*

See how it's possible to offer some value-added advice without being too salesy? A statement like this acknowledges that your prospect is not currently in the market (first sentence) but still demonstrates your expertise, so he will remember and perhaps contact you when he's ready to move.

This model works for consultants, CPAs, accountants, financial planners, coaches—just about anyone in a service-based industry in which knowledge is the main product. The concern we sometimes hear from clients is that their knowledge is valuable and they don't want to just give away their intellectual capital.

We agree. You shouldn't have to. But here's the rub: few people will sign up with you if they're not sure you can do the job—and in the absence of a tangible product, you have nothing but your technical expertise to demonstrate that you have the goods. And when you think about it, that makes sense. Whenever you're ready to buy an automobile, it doesn't matter how much research you've done on a particular model, you're probably not going to write your check until you've taken the car for a test-drive.

The same is true for your prospects. Give them a little test-drive to show how it would feel to do business with you. If you're a marketing consultant, give them a couple of ideas on how they can increase the exposure of their business. Don't go overboard; maybe offer a technique you read in a magazine or tried with one of your clients. Just give them something they can try on to see if it works.

Not only will this open up a good conversation with the person (while you're out networking), but if you play your cards right, whom do you think they'll go to when they're in need of your kind of service? When it comes to building rapport and creating trust, nothing does it better than solid, helpful information provided out of a genuine concern for the other person.

Provide a Referral or Contact

Try to offer a direct referral (someone you know who's in the market for this person's services) or a solid contact (someone who could help in other ways down the road). Let's say you're networking and you run into a person who owns a printing shop. You talk for a while, you hit it off, and even though you don't know of anyone who's looking for this person's selection of print services right now, you'd like to help him out. So you say:

> *You know, Jim, I don't know of anyone who's actively in the market for printing services right now, but I do have someone who I think could be a big help to your business. Her name is Jane Smith, and she's a marketing consultant. I know a lot of her clients need business cards, fliers, and things like that printed, and while I don't know if she has a deal on the table right now, I think you both would really hit it off if you got together.*

You see how easy that was? You stated right upfront you don't know of anyone in the market right now. You then followed up by saying you do know of someone who you think could help and briefly described how. Chances are, this will sound like a good idea to your new contact.

Be careful; you just met this person and don't want to jump the gun by letting him into your contact database too soon. However, in the rare cases where you feel a connection right off the bat, don't be afraid of pointing him in the direction of someone you know who could help his business.

DOWN ON THE FARM

When you're farming for contacts, it means you're focusing more on the relationship itself than on what you might get as a result of knowing this person. It also means that the way you develop your relationship is far more important than anything your fellow networkers bring to the table.

Once you buy into farming as an approach to relationship networking, you'll find yourself

- a lot less stressed, since you won't feel the pressure to get more immediate business at whatever networking function you're at today
- more upbeat, since each networking event won't feel like a hit-or-miss approach for getting more business
- getting more clients than you can possibly handle, as prospects begin to gravitate to your cool, confident aura without even knowing why

So remember, when it comes to farming for contacts, it's about consistency, reliability, and a genuine desire to get to know the other person. Keep those goals in mind, and in no time you'll be networking like a pro.

4

Fishing for Referrals

Do referrals happen by accident?

A few years ago, a long-standing member of a business networking organization was talking about canceling his membership—not because he wasn't getting enough referrals but because he was getting *too much* business.

That's right. Despite a full year of getting great referrals, Steve's friend Mike didn't feel that the results proved that networking was a viable business strategy for getting more referrals. He felt that the business he had gotten was based on "chance occurrences"—one person knowing another, who happened to know him—and despite the fact that he kept getting these referrals *as a result of his networking contacts*, it couldn't possibly last. So he left the group.

Even though Mike's misguided reasoning led him down the wrong road, it raises a good question, and understanding the answer could help your business. The question is simply this: Despite the chance nature of networking, is meeting more people something you can count on as a consistent means of getting more business?

Mike's challenge boiled down to two things: *repeatability* and *understanding.* His training told him that the way to get more business was to target a certain kind of customer by calling people from a demographics-based list. If he didn't have enough business, he needed to make more calls. How many more? He could figure that out, too, because the amount of business he got was directly proportional to the number of people he talked to. It was a repeatable process that he fully understood.

On the other hand, clients he got from referrals always had a story line that he couldn't see being repeated. Sally knew Jim, who ran into Sue, who happened to be in his group and referred Mike the business. This led Mike to conclude that the results were coincidental and couldn't possibly be repeated.

Mike's reasoning wasn't entirely off track, as far as it went. If you focused on the specific people who gave you the referral, rather than the process and relationships that allowed it to happen, then no, you couldn't consistently get more business from networking. Or to put it another way: Sally knowing Jim, who ran into Sue, who ultimately gave Mike a referral is probably never going to happen again in exactly that way. But if you step back and ask, "Is it possible that somebody will know someone else who's looking for my services and will then give me that referral?" well, that's a whole other story—especially if you focus on building relationships so that there's always a *somebody.*

What led Mike astray was this: he was thinking about hunting when he should have been thinking about fishing.

A LONG AND WINDING RIVER

To understand how getting referrals is a lot like fishing, you need to look at the process from a different perspective. When it comes to networking and passing referrals, it's *not* about who's giving what to whom. At no point in this book do we say, "For every referral you give, you can expect one in return." Nor do we say that when you hand out more referrals, other business professionals will automatically do the same. It just doesn't work that way.

Think of referral giving in the context of the abundance mind-set (see Chapter 2), which is the awareness that there's more than enough business to go around. If you hear of a business opportunity that would be well suited for a referral partner—in other words, not your kind of business, but hers—think of it as excess business. When you pass this kind of excess business to others in the form of a referral, you'll wind up attracting more prospects who want to work with you.

Call it an act from the referral gods, but when you do good things for others, those good things have a habit of making their way back to you—often from a different person or group of people. Even if it seems that you're not benefiting from the referrals you're giving to others, take note of all the other business that "just happens" to come your way:

- the guy who stumbles across your website and gives you a call
- the old prospect you haven't heard from in months who suddenly wants to get together for lunch
- the inactive client who wants to renew his contract with you

Even though it seems like happenstance, some or all of that is likely to be new business you attracted by giving away other business (in the form of referrals) to people you know.

NETWORKING WITH A NET

Referral networking is a lot like catching fish by casting a net. Each fish comes to the net by a different path; each has a story that is not repeated. You don't focus on a particular fish and then try to get it to come to the net; in fact, you usually don't even see the fish until you pull in the net. Instead, you focus on the action of setting the net. You know that if you set your net correctly and consistently, fish will eventually come, no matter what path they take to get there.

The same is true for getting referrals. The process of meeting people, staying in touch, and then asking for their business is something you can do time after time. You don't have to worry about how a specific referral got to you, because you understand the process of setting your net.

And here's the best part: Just as with fishing, your net can be working for you all the time. You don't have to be there whenever someone you know runs into someone else who could use your services, which means you can be fishing in many different ponds simultaneously and reaping tons of new business. This is especially true when you've become a referral gatekeeper and have begun to get referrals not only from your own network of contacts but from the networks of others as well.

When it comes to networking, there is no coincidence about referrals. They're the inevitable cumulative result of the day-to-day activities of relationship building. And even though they can't be measured as easily as cold calls, the results are far more powerful.

Throughout this book you'll find the tools to build a rock-solid foundation for profitable business relationships. By the end, you'll have a clear understanding of the entire process that produces referrals, rather than an undue concern over the exact chain of events leading to a specific piece of business. Once you understand that, be warned: you will have more business than you can handle.

PART II

YOUR NETWORKING STRATEGY

5

Three Essential Questions

U p to this point, we've talked about networking in terms of its general principles and mindset. But now we want to shift gears a bit and talk about developing a strategy that can help you jump into networking with both feet—or to put it another way, creating a framework that will help you decide which events you should attend and which you should take a pass on.

Because, let's face it, in most major cities you can attend eight to ten networking events on any given day. Assuming that your minimum time investment is two hours per event (this takes into account getting in the car, driving downtown, parking, and participating in the event), it's easy to see how this networking thing can be a full-time job.

So the question becomes this: How can a time-strapped businessperson figure out which networking events she should attend and which she should let go by the wayside? The answer: by developing a networking strategy.

Most successful companies have a business plan that coordinates the many facets of that enterprise into a coherent document. These companies usually have a marketing plan as well that includes a month-by-month set of actions for getting the word out about the business.

Why not have a networking strategy that helps you plan which events to attend? Here are three easy—but definitely essential—questions you need to answer in order to create a plan that will work for you.

1. WHO ARE MY BEST PROSPECTS?

The first question is another way of asking, "What is my target market?" You'd be surprised at the number of business professionals who can't define their target market. Most of them either reply, "Everyone!" or offer some vague description that sounds good at first but offers little in the way of useful specifics. This is why business professionals so often find themselves running all over town, trying to attend every networking event that comes down the pike. As the George Harrison song says, "If you don't know where you're going, any road will get you there." Since they don't have time to follow up immediately with most of the people they meet, they often don't get as much business as they'd like; then they throw their hands in the air and wail, "Networking doesn't work for me!"

But as a smart, enterprising businessperson, you already know that networking works. It's just a matter of developing a strategy that puts you into contact with the right people.

The *right* people? If you're not sure who those folks might be for your business, go back and take a look at your list of past clients. What industries were they in? How long had they been in business? Were your clients even businesses to begin with, or have you worked mostly with consumers?

As an example, if you're a real estate agent, you might want to meet first-time home buyers and people who are interested in moving downtown. If you're a management consultant, your target audience might be representatives from companies in a specific industry (for instance, medical) or with annual sales greater than a certain figure (say $1 million). Or, if you're an accountant or a CPA, you might be targeting small-business owners—one- or two-person shops that don't have the resources to hire a full-time bookkeeper.

Each one of those is fine, but each target market will have a strategy that requires you to network in different places. Once you've put together a profile of the people you've worked with in the past, pick up the phone and run it by a few trusted friends and colleagues. See what they think. People who are close to you often have insights into patterns that you tend to overlook because you're busy with day-to-day operations, and this is a great time to get their input on who they feel would be a good fit for your business. Once you get that nailed down, you can go on to the next question.

2. WHERE CAN I MEET MY BEST PROSPECTS?

Networking doesn't mean just hopping into the car and attending the next chamber of commerce event. Yes, the chamber and other business associations are excellent means of finding and meeting new prospects, and we recommend them to anyone as a good starting point. But as your business evolves and you begin targeting specific niche markets, there are other venues and opportunities that fall outside the typical networking event. And that's the kind of out-of-the-box thinking we're going to discuss here.

Generally speaking, if you're trying to meet more small-business owners, you should spend time at the chamber of commerce, your local business association, or a referral group. Not only do these groups have exactly the type of audience you want to meet, but with referral groups, and BNI in particular, there's a system in place that will help you help others get more referrals for you.

If you're looking to meet representatives from bigger corporations in your area, we recommend service clubs, nonprofit groups, and volunteer work. Another good way to come into contact with those folks is through homeowners associations, most of which meet at least once a month. It's a great way to get in contact with folks who are in corporations but don't attend typical networking events.

If your business is geared more toward consumers, then getting involved with your kids' events—Little League, Boy Scouts, and so forth—is another good way to meet the right people.

DAVID

I have two kids and am very involved in Boy Scouts. I'll never forget our first camping trip in Alabama. Time spent in activities with the kids was also time spent with the other dads, every one of whom turned out to be a good business contact. One of those contacts later resulted in a profitable business deal. I created more business opportunity on that trip than I would have at home, and that was not even my goal.

BRIAN

I don't have kids myself, but I recently started coaching an eighth-grade boys' basketball team that has absolutely put me into contact with people (read: parents) whom I would never see at a networking event. If you keep in mind that you want to honor the event (don't hand out fliers on the sidelines), that kind of volunteer work will put you in an excellent position to meet more of your target audience.

If you're that real estate agent who wants to meet first-time home buyers and people interested in moving downtown, you'll probably find more prospects by networking at downtown events. It doesn't matter which event, as long as it's being held in the city center. That should bring you into contact with people who might be thinking about moving out of their apartment and getting into a house. Look also for networking events likely to be attended by young professionals, since these are the people most likely to be living in an apartment while accumulating the disposable income to buy a downtown condo or home.

For the management consultant who wants to meet people in million-dollar companies, we'd recommend networking at service clubs or nonprofit groups. Why? Because the directors and CEOs of large companies are less likely to be at your local chamber's after-hours event than in a civic organization like Habitat for Humanity, Kiwanis, or Rotary. We also recommend trying to get on your service club's board or leadership team; that way you're interfacing with more of the movers and shakers of your community. Careful, though: if you're too direct in these clubs, too obviously looking for business relationships, you won't be welcomed. These groups are more civic than business oriented, which means you'll have to establish your credibility through community-oriented activities rather than business deals.

3. WHOM, EXACTLY, DO I WANT TO MEET?

You've heard the assertion that there are six degrees of separation between you and any other person, haven't you? The idea is that, through at most five intermediaries, you can meet anybody on the planet that you choose to. It's a networker's dream of heaven.

The trouble is it just isn't true.

In their book *The 29% Solution,* Dr. Ivan Misner and his co-author, Michelle Donovan, point out that the "six degrees of separation" notion applies to only a small fraction of the population at most. Experiments by sociologist Stanley Milgram in the 1960s and '70s found that, yes, the people who made the desired connection did it through an average of five or six people, but some did it through two connections while others took ten intermediaries or more. But here's the real hitch: only 29 percent were successful in making the connection at all. The overwhelming majority (71 percent) never got through to the intended person! Worse, other studies by Milgram achieved an even more anemic rate of success.

This tells us that most people are not well connected in any practical sense. However, among people who are extraordinarily well connected, you can get in contact with anyone through, on the average, only five intermediaries. The best networkers strive to be among that 29 percent, and our work is to help people join this world of master networkers.

Now, here's an interesting fact that we've noticed: even accomplished networkers sometimes fail to realize that they're closer to a much-desired contact than they imagine. There's a story about two networkers who had worked together closely for many years. One day one of them said to the other, "You know, I've been going to a lot of events lately, but I still haven't been able to meet one guy I really need to see. If I could meet the CEO of LotsaBucks Corporation, I could take it easy for a while. But there's no way I'm going to get a meeting with him by calling."

"There's a trade show next month. Come with me and I'll introduce you."

"You know this guy?"

"Yeah, we've been in the same country club for seven years."

"Why didn't you tell me you knew him?"

"You didn't ask."

The principles behind making this kind of connection—summed up in the simple aphorism "You don't know whom they know"—are ably outlined by Wayne Baker at Humax in a referral tool he calls the Reciprocity Ring. Boiled down to its essentials, the idea is that the greater the number of networks you're connected with, the greater the chance that there's a short chain of contacts between you and anyone you'd care to name. All you have to do is recognize that fact and ask a few people a specific question or two. The answers will either put you in direct contact or lead you in the direction of the networking events you need to attend.

Even if you can't name the people you want to meet, the better you can describe them, the greater the chance that you'll get to meet your ideal contact. The secret ingredient in this principle is specificity. The way to meet the unknown contact is to be as specific as possible without closing out all possible variations. You can do this by starting your question like this: "Whom do you know who . . . ?" You complete the sentence with specifics: "Whom do you know who is a new parent?" "Whom do you know who belongs to an organization that builds houses for the homeless?"

By asking for a specific kind of contact, you focus the other person's attention on details that are more likely to remind him of a specific person than if you asked, "Do you know anyone who needs my services?"

Now, before we paint too rosy a picture on meeting the right people, let us be clear on one thing: senior executives are hiding from you.

Well, maybe not hiding, but you can't expect the director of marketing at a Fortune 1000 company to go out of his way to meet you. Don't worry, it's nothing personal. It's just that he's a

IVAN

The VCP Process® is part of the foundation of relationship networking. You start by being visible—that is, by being at networking events and getting acquainted with a potential referral partner. Credibility comes after you've had dealings with the person and become known to him as someone who does good work and can be trusted. Profitability comes last, after you and your networking partner have established a history of helping each other succeed in business. Depending on the frequency and quality of your contacts and the desire of both of you to develop the relationship, it may take months or even years to progress through these phases, but the payoff is well worth the investment. This simple concept has made a bigger difference in more people's networking efforts than any other single idea I've discussed. When people get this, all the techniques I teach fall into place much more effectively.

very busy person, and it would be literally a full-time job to listen to every Tom, Dick, and Harriet who wants to sell him or his company on some new idea. That's why it's important to surround yourself with quality business contacts, since the best way to your ideal contact very often is through another contact.

It's less of "I'm going to this networking event to find the right prospect" and more of "I'm networking to develop mutually beneficial relationships with people in the local business community." It's a recognition that the development of a mature, mutually beneficial referral relationship follows the VCP Process® through its three stages: visibility, credibility, and profitability.

One of the great things about the growth of referral networking is that there are so many more opportunities available today than there were even five years ago. Unfortunately, there's also a downside: you may quickly feel overwhelmed by the vast number of events in your town and by the whirlwind of networking that seems to characterize most of them. However, when you answer these three key questions and begin creating a strategy, you'll find that the networking world truly is your oyster. All you have to do is put yourself in the ideal position for meeting the people who are most likely to do business with you.

6

The Butterfly Effect

You've probably heard of the "butterfly effect," the idea found in chaos theory that a small change of initial conditions in a system can start a chain of events that results in large-scale alterations of later events—that the flap of a butterfly's wing creates a tiny disturbance in the atmosphere that might later influence the path of a tornado halfway around the globe. Well, the wonder of relationship networking is that it has its own kind of butterfly effect.

IVAN

My recent visit to Necker Island is a vivid demonstration of the butterfly effect—the theory that a small action in one place can have a ripple effect that creates a dramatic action in another place. In networking it is about how a seemingly minor connection or conversation with one person may, after many ripples across the network, end in a high-powered connection later.

It started several years ago when I received a phone call from Kim George, a woman I didn't know then but who has since become a good friend. Kim asked me if I would be willing to help with the creation of an online networking and social capital community. I agreed to participate, because it fit the values and direction I wanted for my company. This was the first flap of the butterfly's wing.

It took time and work to put it together, and our collaboration on this network turned naturally into a strategic alliance, which led to a speaking engagement, which allowed me to meet Jack Canfield, co-author of the *Chicken Soup for the Soul* series. Jack invited me to participate in an international organization, the Transformational Leadership Council. There I met Nancy Salzman, owner of NXIVM (pronounced Nexium) Training. Nancy got my wife, Beth, and me invited to spend five days on beautiful Necker Island, talking with some of the world's most successful financiers, movie producers, and business leaders, including Sir Richard Branson—music mogul, world adventurer, and owner of Virgin Atlantic Airways.

Now do you see the tornado taking shape? Wait, there's more.

Sir Richard is the founder of not only Virgin Atlantic Airways but also Virgin Galactic, the world's first private space travel company. Using a two-stage airplane launch system designed by airplane builder Burt Rutan in Southern California, he plans to ferry private astronauts, science packages, and payloads into suborbital space within the next few years. At the end of our visit on Necker Island, Richard invited us to attend the rollout of this new aerospace system in Mojave, California.

A few months later we were flown from Los Angeles International, via a Virgin America charter plane named *My Other Ride Is a Spaceship*, to the Mojave Spaceport. There in the windswept desert at the base of the Sierra Nevada mountains, we witnessed the unveiling of *WhiteKnightTwo*, the astounding twin-fuselage "mothership" that will carry *SpaceShipTwo* aloft and launch it into space. It was an otherworldly experience.

At the party in Bel Air later that evening, Burt told me that he expects the cost of space tourism to drop to a fraction of its current cost once all the systems are in place. He also expects Virgin Galactic to open a space hotel; that set me thinking about holding business networking meetings in orbit. I told him I thought that was a bold long-term vision. He said, "That's just our midterm vision. Later we'll have private space trips from the earth to the moon and back."

And the tornado goes on spinning. Who knows where it will stop?

Thus a simple telephone call from a fellow networker led me over the course of a few years to a networker's dream—the chance to hobnob with world movers and shakers on a Caribbean island and to see the launching of the private space travel industry. It demonstrates vividly how a seemingly insignificant contact can lead you to connections and relationships that may well surprise you when you look back to where the journey started. When the butterfly flaps its wings, you never know where you'll end up, but if you're on your toes, you can ride the whirlwind to success.

There is one other salient fact about Ivan's butterfly that he did not mention: it raised his value as a networker by at least a few notches. Who wouldn't want to have a networking partner who can connect with Sir Richard Branson, Burt Rutan, and all their connections? You never know whom they know. (Caution: before you ask Ivan for these contacts, make sure you are at the high end of C (credibility) with him. See Chapter 17, "How Deep Is Your Network?" for more on that.)

7

The Four Streams of Your Networking River

Your business strategy comprises multiple elements that work together toward achieving your overall goal, whether that goal is higher sales, greater profit, geographic expansion, or something else. Depending on the type of business you're running, these strategic streams might include a sales plan, a cost-cutting initiative, a training program, and other elements.

In the same way, when you're developing your networking strategy, you need to think of your ideal network as a broad, powerful river being fed by several smaller streams, each providing a distinct set of contacts as well as unique opportunities to make your network deeper, stronger, and more diverse. These streams are very different, just as the Ohio River is different from the Missouri and the Arkansas, but they work together synergistically to create the great Mississippi. Together, they are far more effective at putting you in touch with your best prospects than they would be if you accessed them separately and added up the results. If your network lacks this diversity of sources, it will be far less effective as a business resource.

In this chapter we talk about four of these streams, the four we consider particularly important to have in a well-developed referral network. We don't claim these are the only ones that exist. Some networkers, depending on the nature of their business and their own proclivities and experience, prefer to identify other kinds of organizations, such as women's networking groups and community service organizations, as distinct types. To simplify our discussion, however, we have included these in either the casual-contact or the strong-contact category, depending on their structure and practices.

CASUAL-CONTACT NETWORK

You've probably attended meetings of some general business groups, and in the course of these meetings you've probably met many businesspeople from a wide variety of professions, including competitors in your own field. Such groups typically meet once a month and hold mixers where people mingle and meet informally. There are often guest speakers, special presentations, and activities such as breakfast meetings designed to facilitate networking. They are devoted mostly to discussion of community affairs, political issues, and local business. The primary example of a casual-contact networking organization is the local chamber of commerce.

Because casual-contact organizations are not tailored primarily to help you get referrals, you have to exert some effort to make them work for you. For example, you can volunteer to be a chamber ambassador, a position that doesn't cost you much time but puts you in touch with a lot of people. Sitting on committees helps you get to know members better, especially the ones who devote the most time to the organization and are therefore good candidates to become diligent, conscientious members of your own network. Most of all, you need to attend regularly so you can take advantage of every opportunity to strengthen the relationships you do form.

KNOWLEDGE NETWORK

Professional associations have been around longer than almost any other kind of group, from the medieval guilds to crafts associations to today's professional groups and industry associations. Membership in a group is usually from one specific industry, such as banking, accounting, health services, legal services, or architecture. Some groups limit membership to their own industry; others are open to all, with vendors and others becoming associate members rather than full members. The primary purpose is for the exchange of information and ideas, whether intraindustry or interindustry.

Joining a group that represents an industry other than your own can put you in contact with a concentrated target market, including many top-quality potential contacts. Many of your best current clients, looking for their own competitive edge, may be members of industry associations. Ask them which open-membership groups they belong to, and try to join a few of them. This can give you an opportunity to meet prospects of the same quality as your clients.

Keep in mind, however, that you're not the only person to think of crashing the party. Some of your competitors have probably joined as well, and for the same purpose. Full members sometimes do not like being "sold" by associate members, so be careful in your approach. Remember that a master networker seeks first to help others. Go in with the idea of helping people solve problems and improve their business. By making friends first you will gain customers later, even if they are not the same people.

The other part of your knowledge network should be groups in your own industry. Yes, you'll be rubbing elbows with competitors, but there are advantages. You'll stay abreast of developments in your industry, find out what your competitors are up to, study the competition's brochures and presentations, and discover opportunities to collaborate with competitors whose specialties are different from yours or who need help on a big project.

ONLINE NETWORK

Networking is as old as civilization, and it changes and adapts as the community changes; so, naturally, you would expect networking to show up on the web as soon as the world's second computer went online. This is pretty much what has happened in the last several years. Online business networking systems such as Ecadamy.com, LinkedIn.com, and Facebook.com put businesspeople in instant communication with one another, making it easier than ever before to pass along information, referrals, and time-sensitive opportunities, especially over a great distance.

The main thing that online networking lacks is, with some exceptions, the face-to-face interaction that is so important to developing and deepening relationships. Although teleconferencing is growing in popularity and technical sophistication, there's nothing like sitting down to breakfast or lunch with a contact to deepen a friendship or a business relationship. For this reason, we recommend online networking as an adjunct to traditional networking, to be used after the relationship is established and with the purpose of getting in touch quickly and passing referrals efficiently. Online networking is hard to beat when used for purposes it's best suited for: communicating ideas, sharing knowledge, and raising your visibility to a larger group of contacts.

DAVID

I was asked about five years ago whether online networking would replace face-to-face networking. My response was "Of course not," but I was thinking, "Is it possible? What if it did?"

As it turns out, I was right. Online networking has not replaced in-person networking. Why hasn't it? Because, I believe, there is a magic that happens when you bring a group of people together in the same room or when you are engaged in a one-to-one conversation with someone.

On the other hand, by using the internet you can significantly enhance the success of your networking by getting to the face-to-face part faster. In the past, if someone in your network asked you for a connection, you'd have to go to your card file and laboriously thumb through to find the contact. Now you can search your online networks, and not only can you check to see if you have a direct connection, but you can see whether the contact is currently online and ask for a referral. Pretty powerful!

In a BNI chapter meeting I recently attended, a commercial real estate agent passed around a list of ten companies with the names of contacts he wanted to meet. I did not recognize any of the names, but when I searched my online networks I found I had 1,741 connections to these people!

STRONG-CONTACT GROUP

Organizations whose purpose is principally to help members exchange business referrals are known as strong-contact referral groups. Some of these groups, BNI for example, meet weekly, typically over breakfast; others meet every two weeks or monthly. Most of them limit membership to one member per profession or specialty. If you're a CPA and join a local BNI chapter, then you'll have locked out the competition by joining; no one else can fill the CPA category in that chapter. Each weekly meeting usually lasts about 90 minutes, and you might want to stay another half hour or so to network afterward and solidify your relationships with other members of the group.

Joining a strong-contact referral group is one the best things you can do for your business, provided you're comfortable with two things:

1. *You need to have a schedule that lets you attend most or all of the meetings.* Regular attendance is vital to developing a rapport with the other members of the group and getting to know their businesses. Otherwise, how can you generate a referral for someone if you don't know him or what he does? How is anyone going to get to know you better and generate referrals for your business? Attending every weekly meeting needs to be a priority. The good news is that since most of these meetings are held in the early morning, they won't intrude too much on your day.

2. *You have to buy into the team approach that defines these organizations.* You need to feel comfortable going to a networking event and being on the lookout for prospects who can help other members of your group. This can be counterintuitive for some, since businesspeople are usually focused on their own business. But if you're a real estate agent and you find out that someone just moved into a new home and is no longer in need of your services, you need the presence of

mind to ask about other areas in this person's life where someone else in your group could help (e.g., electrician, handyman, lawn service). This can be a little tricky at first, but the group will be watching what you do—take our word for it. If you're not fulfilling either of those two requirements, either you'll be asked to leave or referrals will stop coming your way.

A good strong-contact networking group typically tracks the amount of business that is conducted. This is an important measurement of its effectiveness. BNI, for example, tallies up the total number of referrals from the previous week, the amount of revenue attached to that total, and a couple of other metrics that give visitors and members alike a sense of how the chapter is progressing. This is vital information; it tells you what kind of return you can expect on your investment. When you consider potential referral groups, find out how they plan to measure your return on investment.

Another type of strong-contact group is the service club. Unlike the more business-oriented groups discussed previously, the service group is not set up primarily for referral networking; its activities are focused on service to the community. However, as a practitioner of the Givers Gain philosophy, the master networker is a natural fit. In the course of giving time and effort to civic causes, you form lasting relationships that broaden and deepen your personal and business networks. If you go in not to benefit but to contribute, the social capital you accrue will eventually reward you in other ways and from other directions—business among them.

FRIENDS ON THE BIG RIVER

Developing and coordinating the four major streams of your networking river is essential for getting the maximum amout of referral-based business possible. Why? Because it gives you many different ways of making new contacts, puts you in touch with other people's networks, and multiplies the power of your networking by making you the link between a number of diverse networks—professionals, salespeople, trade workers, retail business owners—whose combined reach is broader and richer in coverage than any single group. It will reach beyond the horizon and from the ground to the sky.

Now, here's one more element in this river that we didn't mention earlier, one in which you will find yourself in mutually beneficial contact with more than any other part of your network. Close around you, like the knights around King Arthur's Round Table, will be your most trusted and intimate friends, colleagues, and family members. The most successful networkers usually have 6 to 12 people in their inner circle, relationships that have come from any or all of the streams of their network (see Figure 7.1). The deep relationships with these strong contacts bring them most of the business they need and provide a steady, high-quality supply of new contacts and prospects. Referrals from outside this inner circle are simply icing on the cake.

Once you've established this inner circle, make it a priority to meet with a member of that group at least once every other month. That way you won't lose touch with any of them, and they'll always be on top of what's going on with your business.

Figure 7.1

Four Major Networking Streams

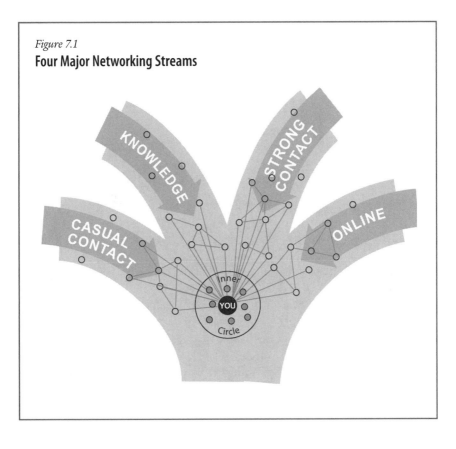

CHAPTER

8

Where Networkers Gather

Business professionals who don't have a lot of spare time on their hands often ask us which networking groups provide the biggest bang for their buck. We tell them that there are five main types, and that what works best depends on the business they're in and the prospects they want to meet. Here's a quick rundown of the most familiar types.

Organization	Type
Chamber of commerce	Casual contact
Business association	Casual or strong contact
Service club	Strong contact
Referral group	Strong contact
Social network for business	Online network

CHAMBER OF COMMERCE (CASUAL CONTACT)

The chamber of commerce is considered the bedrock of local networking, and it is represented in almost every business community. The chamber's main mission is to facilitate the growth of local small businesses, and generally speaking you'll find a wide range of businesspeople attending these events—everyone from coaches and consultants to florists and real estate agents.

People usually gravitate toward the chamber closest to their place of work (or home), making it a very easy place to find business owners who are clustered geographically. This is particularly good for business professionals who have retail presence within the city, since networking at the chamber puts them into contact with the people most likely to frequent their physical location. If you're a restaurant owner, community banker, or even country club representative, you should seriously consider hosting a chamber networking event at your location. Chambers of commerce are constantly looking for wide-open venues, and considering that most chambers hold six to ten events each year, there's no shortage of opportunities for finding an event that works best for you.

Another good thing about the chamber is the sheer number of people you'll meet. There are generally anywhere from 30 to 100 people at every event. That might not be a lot compared with other conferences you attend, but for a local networking event

BRIAN

I have an attorney client who hosted an event right outside her office. (She works in the historic part of town, so her place of business is set up more like a house than a typical office park.) Her firm hired a band and ordered food, and from what I understand everyone had a great time. Needless to say, they were getting referrals from that event long after it was over. So, if you have a business with a suitable physical location, I'd definitely recommend hosting an event.

it's a pretty good number. Obviously, attendance varies from city to city, but you'll rarely see a chamber event with fewer than 30 people.

Here's why we consider a chamber of commerce to be a casual-contact networking group. You'll see a bunch of people all at the same time, but your odds of seeing the same people every week are pretty slim. This isn't necessarily a problem, but it does make chamber networking different from that of other groups we'll talk about.

In terms of membership, for an annual commitment you're usually looking at an investment roughly equivalent to the cost of a nice suit. Depending on the city, that should get you some space in the chamber's yellow pages, a ribbon-cutting ceremony, plus a discounted rate for attending its regular networking events—and if you're lucky, some space on its website. All in all, the chamber is definitely a good first step for networking with new people and getting the word out about your business.

BUSINESS ASSOCIATION
(CASUAL OR STRONG CONTACT)

A business association is a close cousin to the chamber in that they are both set up along geographic lines. The only problem with networking events sponsored by business associations is that they're usually set up along city lines, as opposed to county lines with the chamber, which means you might find fewer people attending those events. However, that's not necessarily a bad thing; depending on your experience, a smaller group can provide a more manageable number of people to meet (and relationships to deepen).

The types and number of establishments are also different with a business association. A chamber of commerce tends to draw a higher concentration of service professionals, such as insurance agents, bankers, and consultants, and your local business association usually draws restaurant owners, fitness club providers, and other small retail businesses. Depending on whom you're trying to meet and how long you've been networking, this can work in your favor.

Let's imagine that you're a new businessperson who's just getting her feet wet with this whole networking thing. Attending a business association event is a great start. There's probably one located pretty close to where you live, and you'll have a relatively small crowd to talk to. This way you don't have to worry about being intimidated by meeting a bunch of new people.

If you own a retail store, a business association event will put you into contact with people who probably pass by your store every day. Membership costs are usually nominal. It's wise to do a little research and see what's available, but either way, this is a useful, if small, step for getting the word out about your business.

SERVICE CLUB (STRONG CONTACT)

Groups like Rotary, Lions, and Kiwanis are organized around the advancement of a service-oriented cause. The Kiwanis Club, for example, is "a global organization of volunteers dedicated to changing the world one child and one community at a time." This simply means that during the group's weekly meetings, the overarching theme will be helping the kids in your community through volunteering at the local high school, holding a fundraiser, or conducting similar projects.

We consider service organizations strong-contact networking groups. There are weekly meetings, attended by mostly the same people, closely connecting in a common interest: contributing to their community. Often these groups meet on Saturday mornings for a volunteer project or work with other groups in a community fundraiser. Either way, service club members generally have many opportunities for strong-contact networking.

Now here's the thing about service clubs: Their objective is less about sales and getting new business than about helping the people and the community at large. During their meetings you'll discuss specific community projects related to the mission of your group, as opposed to learning the latest business-building techniques as you would from a speaker at the chamber of commerce.

For networking, this is a plus. It stresses long-term relationships and community involvement, which should be at the top of your list as a businessperson trying to get more business through networking. However, don't be surprised if you don't get any business from this group the first year (Gasp!).

As a matter of fact, that's usually the case, because the other members are understandably wary of new members. They're leery of people who swoop in, grab some business, and fly out again. Rather than give you their business right away, they'll hold off and watch what you do. Think of it as a test to see if you're really in it for the long haul.

Now, before you start crossing service clubs off your list because of the longer lag time, remember this: That longer time frame for generating new business is also the main reason why some people in your industry don't attend these groups. As a matter of fact, a good bit of your competition has steered away from service clubs for that very reason. So there's a good chance that you'll be one of only a couple of people in your industry who visit that 30- to 70-member chapter.

This is great news for financial planners, CPAs, real estate agents, mortgage brokers, and others in hypercompetitive industries where consumers have a hard time distinguishing between two service providers. Take a look at kiwanis.org (Kiwanis Club) and see if you can swing by for a meeting one afternoon. Then put on your community service hat and get to work.

REFERRAL GROUP (STRONG CONTACT)

Referral groups are designed specifically to generate new business for their members through a strong-contact networking process. Here's how it works: The typical chapter consists of 20 to 30 businesspeople or sales reps who meet once a week to pass referrals. The members of the group are usually business and sales professionals such as the local insurance agent, the town florist, a lawyer, a chiropractor, and a printer.

The sole purpose of this group is to enable and encourage members to pass along referrals to other members. So if you were out networking and heard that someone needed help with her website, then you would chat up that person a bit, listen to her issues, and recommend the services of that web designer who's a member of your group. You wouldn't have to sell the web designer to the person you just met, but you'd have to know enough about the web designer's business to properly explain how he might be able to help this new person. (Don't worry about how you'll do that, because most good referral groups will train you to do it.)

Think of referral groups as a mini sales force, with people scouring the community to pass on referrals to your business. That's a pretty powerful marketing device!

With so much going for it, you're probably wondering why everyone isn't a member of a referral group. The answer is what distinguishes referral groups from all others: only one representative of each kind of business is allowed to join a chapter, so there can be no professional competition within the group. That is, there can be only one insurance person, one florist, one consultant, and so on.

Allowing only one membership per industry can be bad news for mortgage brokers and real estate agents, whose industry slots fill up the fastest. For everyone else, though, it shouldn't be too hard to find an open group. As a matter of fact, it's a great idea to visit several referral groups in your area, since not all groups are created equal. If you're an experienced business owner looking for some innovative ways to get the word out about your products or services, check out some of your local referral groups.

We recommend looking into BNI (Business Network International), the largest business networking organization worldwide. In our opinion, BNI offers the best blend of consistency, results, and training to help members get the biggest return on their investment. But don't just take our word for it. Compare BNI with some other groups and see what you think.

SOCIAL NETWORK FOR BUSINESS (ONLINE)

Computer technology and the growth of the internet have made it easier than ever before to connect with large numbers of people. Online networking gives you broad reach at low cost and effort. What it doesn't do, however, is provide a forum where relationships can deepen naturally. The nature of the medium strips out communication cues such as facial expression, tone of voice, and body language, restricting communication to the verbal. This is why emoticons were invented—to help convey whether one is happy :D, angry):o, or perhaps just joking ;). Text messaging on mobile phones is even dicier; sometimes THX C U L8R just doesn't do it for gratitude.

Online networking has a rude etiquette all its own. Communications are more direct and blunt, and less polite, and this often comes across as aggressiveness. It's easy to get "flamed" online—that is, encounter open hostility—when you're chatting or messaging invisibly behind the curtain of cyberspace. In person, social norms dictate more restraint. This is one reason it's better to use online networking with people only after you've established a relationship with them by traditional means. To develop trust, respect, and true friendship, it's hard to beat in-person conversation and the occasional handshake or pat on the shoulder.

There are several ways online networking through a site such as Ecademy.com, LinkedIn.com, or XING.com can contribute to your networking. You can post topics on threads that deal with your area of expertise, and respond to others' postings, to establish a reputation as a knowledgeable expert (see Chapter 22). You can use online bulletin boards in much the same way. Don't join too many online communities or you'll spread yourself too thin to be effective.

If you're already part of an offline networking group, you can create a regional or national club or subcommunity online for the members of your group. This will expand the amount of networking you can do within your own organization.

Blogging (shortened from *web logging*, keeping an online interactive personal journal) is a popular way to create a buzz around your name and establish a cyberspace presence. You can use a blog to discuss issues relating to your industry or specialty, or as a newsletter to post news or an information or opinion column. (A good blog on networking, with plenty of free content, can be found at NetworkingEntrepreneur.com.)

Within your own company, you can take advantage of the internet to publish and distribute an e-mail newsletter to clients,

IVAN

I belong to several online networks. Recently, a networker I didn't know sent this email to me and many others concerning a new member of his group: "Letting her join was the biggest mistake you will ever make. . . . She is a disaster, totally unreliable, a total liar."

I was amazed that this stranger would send me such an offensive email. He would never have had the temerity to say these things face-to-face. If he had behaved like this at an in-person meeting, he'd have been thrown out. Lurking in the shadows of the internet, however, this coward was emboldened by his faceless anonymity.

Whether you're networking in person or online, you're dealing with real people; the basics of etiquette and emotional intelligence should always be observed. You may feel more powerful because you can say anything and send it to many people, but it's not always a good idea.

I e-mailed him back: "I don't know the woman you're talking about, but your email tells me a lot about you. I do not want to receive this kind of slanderous information from you again."

He shot back: "I don't know who you are, but I don't want to talk to nobodies like you."

As another networker reminded me, "Never mud wrestle with a pig. You can only end up muddy—and besides, the pig likes it." I decided not to encourage this nutcase, so I didn't reply. But I did get word to his network administrator that somebody was abusing the privileges of the forum. Appropriate action was taken.

customers, friends, associates, and employees. It should cover a broad range of topics of interest to your audience; you can invite contributions from your readers. This is a good way to strengthen your relationships and increase the number of referrals they bring in.

9

Online Networking:
Click Here to Connect

We talked about the importance of networking via the internet in previous chapters, but let's take a deeper look at what this exploding phenomenon might mean for you—and for traditional business networking itself.

For the record, we believe in online networks. We also believe online networking is not a panacea and that anyone who wants to network like a pro should include it as one of her core strategies—but not rely on it solely. Online networking has strengths and weaknesses. You have to be aware of both its upside and its downside to use it most effectively.

From the most veteran networkers to the newest newbies, questions about web-based opportunities and platforms abound. Could online networking replace face-to-face contacts? Does online networking differ from face-to-face networking in certain key aspects, besides the obvious fact that contact is made through a computer? Who is best suited to online networking? The list goes on.

LOOKING PAST THE HYPE

Before we address those questions and more, allow us a few observations. The wow factor of new social networking techniques and technologies has grabbed people around the world in ways we couldn't have imagined a few short years ago. From politicians and celebrities, to grandmothers and grandchildren, sites like Facebook and Twitter and others have transformed the way many people reach out and communicate.

From our perspective, online communication is here to stay, but it won't stay still. It's dynamic. It's evolving. And it's democratic, with a small *d*, in that online networking literally flattens the communication hierarchy. It enables you to bypass many different organizational levels and filters to communicate with—or jump over—all levels, from top to bottom, making a CEO directly accessible to a temp toiling away in the supply room.

It's pretty exciting stuff. After all, most of us love new toys, no matter what our age! They're fun. They're novel. They sometimes help us attract new friends into our circle, especially if the toy can be shared.

Now, we're not about to claim that online networking platforms are toys. Far from it. But, you have to admit, there are some beguiling parallels: fun . . . novel . . . attract new friends. The line between playful interaction and business-building camaraderie can get blurry—all the more so on the web, where it's often easy to waste more time at a faster rate than in the offline world.

Our point: Avoid getting carried away by all the e-buzz. Hype is kind of like the fluffy meringue on a pie: yummy and fun, but no substitute for a nutritious meal.

Because humans tend to be social creatures and love new toys, we're not surprised that technology today lets us socialize and play in new ways. Understandable enthusiasm for the latest MyBiz FaceSpace site, however, will turn out to be nothing more than an e-distraction unless you have clear purposes in mind for its use.

MIND THE FUNDAMENTALS

How do we stay on track, keeping our business acumen sharp, while nodding knowingly at the sirens of social networking? The best compass for online navigating is the simple, old-fashioned notion "Know thyself." Go back to basics: What do you want from networking? What are you willing to put into your network relationships?

The fundamentals of networking apply—in spades—online. The three stages of the VCP Process—visibility, credibility, and profitability—are as relevant in the online world as they are in face-to-face networking. If you try to bypass the first two stages and get to profitability first, you produce something nobody likes or respects: spam!

There's a confidence curve you have to negotiate before trying to do business with someone. If you take that curve too fast, you'll flip your reputation and end up in a very awkward position. This is especially hazardous in the online realm, because a few words on a computer screen can be interpreted entirely differently than in a face-to-face setting.

IS FACE-TO-FACE COMMUNICATION OUTMODED?

One of the questions we encounter regularly from networkers and would-be networkers is this: Now that we have [fill in the blank with the online social networking space of your choice], doesn't that spell the end of traditional, face-to-face networking? Our answer: No!

As we said in Chapter 7, online communication is a great tool to integrate into your networking, but online doesn't replace face-to-face contact. There are aspects of networking that are simply better face to face: you can see an expression, hear a tone of voice, shake a hand. The nuances of communication and personality conveyed through face-to-face interaction just don't translate well online.

Although every now and then you might encounter people who have a little video camera and phone mic installed on their computer to enable audiovisual two-way communication, most people aren't there yet—and even that setup would not satisfactorily replace face-to-face contact. If you've ever tried teleconferencing, you've seen how it lacks the energy and focus of an in-person meeting. Cheaper than a plane ticket? Sure, but no substitute for a good networking event.

Business networking is about relationships—hopefully, relationships that lead to reciprocal gain—and because relationships depend on both verbal and nonverbal language, face-to-face contact is irreplaceable. Business-building relationships require depth, trust, and a real understanding of participants' needs, wants, and expectations.

CONNECTING WITH PEOPLE AT WEB SPEED

The best online network developers understand very clearly how important and irreplaceable face-to-face contact is in business. For example, Ecademy.com founders Penny and Thomas Power hit the nail on the head with the description they use on their site of how online networking functions for business: "Ecademy enables business people to connect through online networking, at

IVAN

While I was in Stockholm giving a presentation on networking, a Swedish newspaper reporter arranged to do an interview with me. I agreed, and when he arrived for the interview he really started putting me on the spot about online networking, telling me it was replacing face-to-face contact. He was pretty militant about his point of view, and was essentially telling me that traditional networking was going the way of the buggy whip.

Well, I was a little annoyed and surprised that this reporter was being kind of confrontational about networking. So I finally asked him: "Why are you here to do this interview?"

He seemed confused and asked, "What do you mean?"

I said, "Why did you drive all the way out here to this big stadium to meet with me in person just for this interview?"

He looked at me and said, "Interviews are better face to face."

And I said, "Exactly! I rest my case."

"Networking is much the same," I told him. "It beats communicating online, or over the phone, because nothing can ever fully replace an in-person conversation."

The reporter relented. "Yeah, I get it," he said. "That makes sense. Some things are much better in person."

business networking events and 1-2-1 meetings—a community that advocates, connects, and helps one another."

That Ecademy example is a great way to illustrate one of our key points: An online platform is a means to an end. Online networking is a tool to enhance offline networking. The online piece helps networking occur—among real people.

Online technologies do facilitate quick and convenient communication. Ivan and his staff at BNI use a service called Ping.fm, which enables them to distribute one message simultaneously to

IVAN

Ecademy is one of my favorite online networks, because it's one-to-one online and in person. You can actually meet people as well as communicate via the internet. Ecademy has online forums that are very active. They also do regional meetings and encourage members to meet around the world.

Those forums are like turbochargers for your online networking. They really empower two-way communication. I can do a public blog post, for example, and get tens of thousands of hits—and a few comments. On Ecademy's forums, though, I might get a few hundred hits but dozens and dozens of comments. You get more actual responses in a forum than on a blog. So, the engagement level tends to be higher on online networks like Ecademy. They're another great touch point.

Facebook, Twitter, Plaxo, LinkedIn, and a panoply of other social networking sites. He and his staff send four or five quotes a week via Ping, which spares them from having to log onto all of those sites separately—a huge time saver.

Similarly, Ivan and his team use RSS feeds (*RSS* is short for *real simple syndication*) from his blog to push updates out to his pages on Facebook, LinkedIn, and others. That way, people who have opted in as his friends can get the feed quickly and automatically.

IVAN

These technologies let you communicate directly with people who are interested in hearing what you have to say. My friends—the members of my audience—are all over the world, so I can say something that I want to communicate globally and get the message out in the blink of an eye.

Systems like Ping and RSS represent the 21st-century version of the 19th-century telegraph, except you don't need a guy at the other end to decode your message, write it down, then run around town looking for its intended recipient. This modern model instantly gets the message out to everyone who wants it—no middleman, no filter, no hierarchy to navigate.

That unfiltered, unfettered messaging efficiency presents a big risk, though, as we noted earlier. The fact that online networking flattens communication means that the VCP Process can more easily be abused. Because it's such an easy way to communicate, online networking presents a big temptation to ignore the visibility and credibility steps and cut straight to profitability. So, please remember: the social and emotional aspects of networking don't change just because the communication is online.

Despite all its charms, we don't think technology will replace face-to-face networking until we can have meetings like, oh, the Jedi Knights in *Star Wars*. We'll probably look like Yoda by then, and we'll see our Luke Skywalkers and Princess Leias networking holographically; networking groups will be operating in galaxies far, far away. And, hey, if all that happens, it'll be really amazing, but we have a hunch we're not going to see it in our lifetime.

IS ONLINE NETWORKING A GOOD FIT FOR YOU?

Who is best suited for online networking? On the one hand, the answer is obvious: Anyone with a computer and an internet connection (preferably broadband) can access the growing number of social networking sites on the web.

The less obvious answer, however, is based on you and your interactive and time management preferences. Do you enjoy spending time on your computer? Some personality types avoid computer-based interactions as much as possible, while others seem drawn to their monitors like moths to light bulbs. There's no right or wrong about it, just degrees of preference. The more you like browsing the internet, communicating via e-mail, and otherwise working on your computer, the more likely you are to find online networking a good fit.

If online living isn't your thing, don't despair. Remember, web-based networking is a means to an end. A little time online can be leveraged to great effect when you use that time for connecting briefly with new contacts you'd like to meet in person or for following up after face-to-face encounters.

Consider in advance how much of your time—as in how many hours per day or week—you are truly willing to devote to online networking, as well as how you prefer to use that time (i.e., reviewing discussions in online forums, keeping your profiles updated, posting to your blog, reading and responding to comments, reading other people's blogs, tweeting on Twitter, and so on).

Which online networking platform is best for you? Many are available, so pick the one(s) where your target audience hangs out most. We think very highly of a few sites in particular: Ecademy.com, LinkedIn.com, Plaxo.com, and XING.com. There are others, such as EntrepreneurConnect.com and FastPitch Networking.com, that are newer but very good. All of these communities are geared to business networking, and all the authors of this book participate in some or all of these social networks.

Although sites like MySpace and Facebook tend to be more social, we've actually found that Facebook is a reasonably good way to stay in touch. In fact, if you're building a community of people who are following you, then Facebook and Twitter are great tools for that. If you're just starting to build your community, a platform like LinkedIn is a good place to begin the process.

We recommend that you get to know the expectations, customs, and attitudes of your online community before wading in too deep or upgrading to a site's paid version (where applicable). If you plan to spend lots of time online, you might try a few networks. If you want your time online to be minimal, focusing on the one that best fits your needs will prove more comfortable and effective. No matter how many sites you're active on, be very clear with yourself—and with others—about your motives and goals. Stay positive, informative, and value oriented.

Learn the difference between interactions that move you and your online community members toward productive relationship building and those that simply suck time and energy. For example, if someone asks a question that you can answer, that's an opportunity to be helpful while displaying your knowledge. Be careful, though, when comments veer into opinion, because you can easily make an offhand remark that goes viral (i.e., spreads quickly online)—and that you will regret within seconds. There's no pulling something back once it's in cyberspace, and the audience for your unintended remark can grow exponentially.

Above all, as with any kind of business networking, your objective is to develop social capital. Here's a question you'll have to confront in the online world: Will your investment of time, energy, and caring on behalf of other networkers be reciprocated in ways that you find meaningful? Only you can define what *meaningful* means to you, and only you can decide whether your investment is productive.

OTHER WAYS TO COMMUNICATE WITH YOUR E-NETWORK

As we noted in Chapter 8, blogging and e-newsletter publishing can complement your online networking. Both can also be time-consuming, as the material must be updated regularly to remain current—both in content and in the minds of your audience. So, proceed carefully and deliberately if you choose to launch either or both of these communication tools.

A blog offers your audience a place to get to know you better, but it works as intended only if your target audience itself spends the time to read it. The best blogs are written with their readers (as opposed to their authors) in mind and fill a specific need. For example, blogging about your thoughts on foreign policy works only if you happen to be involved somehow in foreign affairs and can write authoritatively for an interested audience. Blogging about what you had for lunch today will probably interest people only if you are a restaurant critic or at least writing for an audience of ardent foodies.

Books and websites on blogging abound, so educate yourself before diving in. Check out the three biggest blog platforms—Blogger.com, Typepad.com, and WordPress.com—for resources and guidance. But use caution: A blog is so easy to start today that you could fall into the "ready, fire, aim" trap and get sidetracked into an activity that ends up being a tangent rather than a core strategy of your online networking.

Publishing an e-newsletter likewise could add to, or distract from, the pursuit of your online goals. Much of what we said about blogging applies equally to electronic newsletters: Know your audience and what it wants. Write for your readers and not for yourself.

Know *why* you're publishing it, too. Are you hoping to sell your products or services, build your brand, keep people coming back to your website, alert readers to the latest developments in your company, or fill an information gap? E-mail newsletters can help you engage with your target audience and generate support and interest—when they're well conceived and well executed.

Decide on your newsletter's frequency in advance. If you're not sure about certain elements of it, start with monthly so you can learn as you go without inflating expectations. Increasing the frequency to satisfy audience demand is much better than having to decrease frequency because of low interest or other problems.

Publishing an e-newsletter requires decent writing skills, the willingness and ability to learn the ropes (i.e., software, design and formatting, collecting and managing e-mail addresses), and a long-term commitment to getting out a quality issue on time, every time.

A CORE STRATEGY THAT'S WORTH KNOWING

As one of the four streams of your networking river, the online world stands to play a growing role in your own VCP Process, regardless of how many hours you want to devote to web-based networking. Becoming comfortable and conversant with it will enhance your ability to at least discuss the issues involved with fellow networkers. Ideally, online networking can serve as one of your core community-building strategies, as long as you look past the hype and focus clearly on your own goals, as well as on the living, breathing people clicking away on the other side of your internet connection.

10

Developing Your Target Market

By this stage in the strategy planning process, you've identified the major components of the broad, deep network you hope to establish. You've studied the different types of networking organizations and how they fit into your overall strategy. You've identified the types of businesspeople that make up your target market.

Now we're ready to look at the final pieces of the strategic puzzle. The first of these is you: How do you fit into your own strategy? Second, where will you find the people you want to interact with and make part of your network?

To start, let's identify some of the strengths and skill sets that you bring to the table as a business professional.

- Are you a "people person"?
- Do you enjoy public speaking?
- What kind of professional background did you have *before* starting your business?
- How long have you lived in the area where you do business?
- What other natural skills do you have (such as time management, staying organized, keeping clients focused) that don't fall directly into your business expertise but are valued by people?

Once you've got that written down, ask yourself, "What group of people or target market is best suited for my services?"

As an example, if you're an extraverted consultant who worked for a big insurance company before starting your own business, then insurance companies, and maybe even their agents, would be a terrific target market for you. A group like this would value the expertise you bring to the table, and by leveraging your previous work experience, you'd be able to talk in a language they'd understand. You'd probably have great success closing the deal when engaging these prospects.

A great place for you to network would be any insurance trade association that met in your area. Health insurance, property and casualty insurance—you name it, there's an association for it. So, instead of spending your time in places where insurance professionals might or might not be, you could focus your networking energies on attending events where your target market shows up in force.

As another example, let's say you're a real people person who dabbles in public speaking. Your services lend themselves to small to medium-size firms—fewer than ten employees—and you're looking for places to meet them. Because speaking is one of your strengths, part of your networking strategy could be delivering a presentation at your local chamber of commerce or business association. That's a great way to meet a lot of people at once, and it's something we recommend to our clients who want to interface with the small-business market.

Take it a step further. Look at the industry groups you've had the most success with in the small-business market, and start networking at their monthly trade association events. Now you're speaking in front of your target market at the chamber, and you're meeting them individually at their industry-specific networking events. For saturating your target market, this would be hard to beat.

People have told us, "Well, that sounds great, but I don't want to limit my prospect base by talking to only one group of people." Fair enough. As business professionals ourselves, we know how hard it seems to get new business. So the last thing you want to do is feel that you're networking to just one group.

BRIAN

I was doing a presentation in North Carolina a few years back for a group of recruiters and staffing companies. Times were tough. The economy wasn't doing so well and businesses simply weren't hiring a lot of staffing or recruiting companies.

When I walked into the room there were about 30 people present, all but 1 of them coming from recruiting and staffing agencies. You know who the other person was? An insurance agent who targeted staffing and recruiting companies as a niche market. Apparently he'd made the business decision some time back to target that particular group, and he'd been networking with them ever since.

Whom do you think 80 percent of those recruiters and staffing company folks used for their insurance needs? You got it—that one insurance agent. I'm sure staffing and recruiting companies weren't his only target market (it's better to have two to three), but even if they were, there had to be several other chapters within driving distance of his business. Couple that with the state, regional, and annual conferences all trade associations have, and you can see that this insurance agent could have had his hands full while networking only with people who were in his target market.

However, when you establish two or three target markets that leverage the inherent strengths of your company and focus your networking there, what you'll find is that your prospects will start calling *you* with their business. Why? Because you obviously know your stuff and are willing to spend some time to get to know them.

Building your business is all about leveraging your strengths within the context of your prospects' needs, then networking with as many of those people as you can. It might mean talking with some of your friends and family ("Hey, I'm rolling out a new program that has me talking to a lot of business equipment companies. Would you happen to know of a person who works for a business equipment firm here in town?"). It might also mean attending every industry-specific association meeting within a

50-mile radius of your office. Or it could be both. But what it *doesn't* mean is running all over town, networking with anyone who happens to be in the room. That's sure to be an exhausting way to acquire new business. A successful business creates a network that is an inch wide and a mile deep, not a mile wide an inch deep.

Start by identifying your strengths: What do you and your business bring to the table? Then determine which group of people would be most receptive to your message; they are your target market. After that, figure out where those folks are most likely to hang out, then focus most of your networking time in those areas. It's as simple as that.

PART III

NETWORKING FACE TO FACE

11

Joining the Crowd

I f you've never before attended a networking event, you may be a little nervous about your first time. That's only natural. The room will be full of people who will be mostly strangers to you, and you'll notice right away that most of them will seem to know other attendees—some of them will seem to be acquainted with every-body!—and will be engaged in lively conversations. Unless you're the most gregarious person on the planet, you'll have some but-terflies at the idea of going in and meeting all these new people.

Although it's natural to be nervous, be reassured that it would be hard to find a more open, inviting group of people than a gathering of business networkers. These are men and women who delight in meeting new people and welcoming them into their networks. Most are just naturally interested in people, and every new face represents a potential new relationship as well as a richer personal, social, and business experience down the line.

But when you go to a mixer or other informal gathering, your first glimpse of the room may be daunting. You'll be confronted with a room full of strangers busily involved in conversations. If you were a fly on the chandelier, you might see something like the scenario in Figure 11.1.

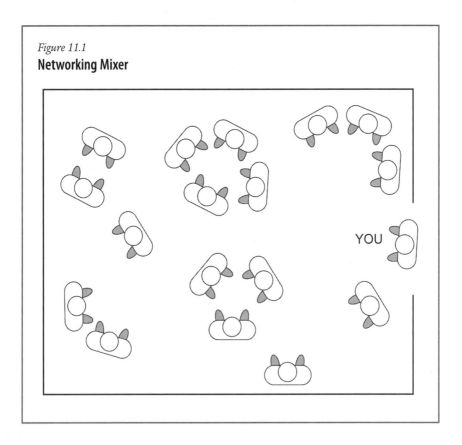

Figure 11.1
Networking Mixer

YOU

You'll see that conversations are going on in clusters of two, three, four, or more people in Figure 11.1. As a stranger, you may feel that if you try to join any of the clusters, you will be intruding. It's an awkward moment, and you may not know quite what to do or where to start.

But take a closer look. The clusters are different, and not just in the number of people in them. The way the groups are configured can tell you a lot about how you will be received if you approach them. Notice, for instance, that some of the groups are configured like those in Figure 11.2.

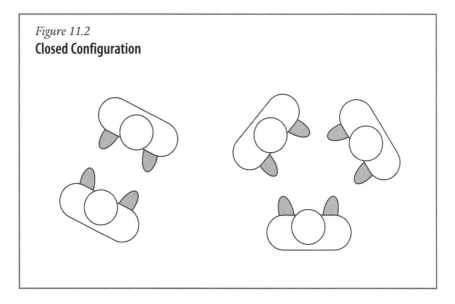

Figure 11.2
Closed Configuration

The people in the Figure 11.2 group, a closed two and a closed three, are facing inward, away from the rest of the room. They are engaged in private conversations. No matter which direction you approach from, their backs are turned to you. These groups are closed, at least for the moment. Unless you like awkward pauses or hostile glares, don't try to force yourself in.

Others clusters look more like those in Figure 11.3.

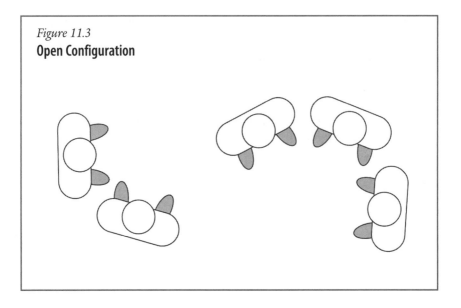

Figure 11.3
Open Configuration

These groups, exemplified here by an open two and an open three, have left an open side from which you can approach them face to face. This orientation is a welcoming configuration; it signals that their conversation is not private and that you would be welcome to join them and introduce yourself.

If you watch for a few minutes, you'll see groups open and close; this is an outward sign of the ebb and flow of the conversation. When a closed group opens, it means there is a break in the intensity of the conversation, or at least in its privacy. Some of the participants may be looking around the room, getting ready either to move or to accept new people into the cluster. That's a good time to join, because it often means the conversation has slowed down or come to a halt and they're ready for a fresh topic—or a fresh face.

As you enter the room, here's what your awareness of these cluster dynamics should be telling you (refer to Figure 11.4). Groups that are closed, like A, B, and C, are probably engaged in private conversations and are not good places to introduce

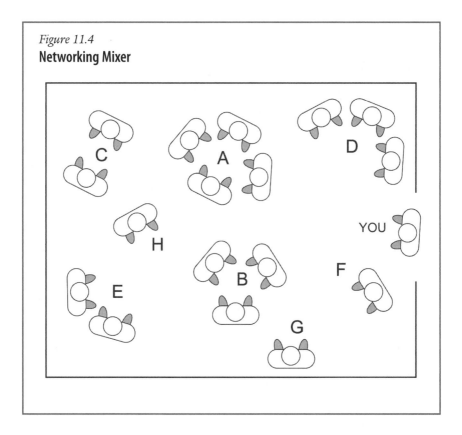

Figure 11.4
Networking Mixer

yourself at the moment. Person F, who entered the room just ahead of you, is heading straight for Person G, who apparently knows him. They probably have some things to say to each other. Don't join them immediately; wait until you see whether they form an open two or a closed two.

Groups that have an open side, like D and E, are implicitly welcoming you to join them. Slide in and listen for a while until you can unobtrusively join the conversation. The others will probably smile and introduce themselves, and you will have started the process of making new friends. Person H, on the other hand, seems to be standing by himself for the moment; this might be a good opportunity to walk up and immediately introduce yourself.

Some of the people who attend a mixer stay grouped together for the entire event. However, if you watch these fixed groups closely, you will see that they open and close from time to time. Other groups break up and re-form in different combinations. Watch and be ready to move to a new open group or to introduce yourself to new people who join the group you're in. You will soon get the feel of the room and will be comfortable navigating from one group to another. Before long the new person coming through the door will see you and think you are the most popular networker in the room.

Learning how to read a crowd, whatever its size, and gauge when to join a group of people who are networking is an acquired skill. Without it, you might find such gatherings daunting and, after unsuccessfully wandering through a few, decide that networking events are not your game.

Nothing could be further from the truth. Networking is a contact sport. You've got to put yourself out there, get into the mix, to become a good networker. In order to make those connections, you need to be able to gauge the warmth of the groups you see at a mixer.

It's still a long journey from fresh face to master networker, but being able to read a room will certainly get you through that daunting first meeting. You may even find it so enjoyable that you'll be not only ready but eager to show up at the next one.

12

The 12 x 12 x 12 Rule

Perception is reality.

How many times have you heard that saying? Probably enough to know that the way you're perceived really does affect the business you conduct (or don't conduct) with other people. This is especially true when it comes to networking and meeting someone for the first time, and this is where the 12 x 12 x 12 rule becomes so important.

What exactly is the 12 x 12 x 12 rule? Basically, it involves three questions:

1. How do you look from 12 feet away? Do you look the part?
2. How do you look from 12 inches away? Are you as good up close as you were from afar?
3. What are the first 12 words out of your mouth?

What we're talking about is perception versus reality, and how important it is to create the right perception of yourself and your business.

Let's face it: As a businessperson, you've got a lot going on. There are people to see, places to go, and a whole lot of stuff to do. Can you do all this, and look and act presentable at all times, too? Quite frankly, it can be a little overwhelming for even the sanest of people.

To complicate things further, most prospects don't care how much you've got going on or how many balls you've got in the air. They just want to know if you can help them solve problems, and the way you look sends signals about how well you can cope.

The same is true for referral partners. They want to know if you have your act together so you won't jeopardize their good name when they refer business to you. Right or wrong, their initial perception of you is going to play a large part in answering that question.

This is precisely what the 12 x 12 x 12 rule is all about. It looks at you from the perspective of other people (prospects or referral partners) and shows you how to optimize their perception.

This does not mean manipulating or deceiving them; experienced people can see through that. Nor is it about checking your personality at the door. What it does mean is fine-tuning your networking practices to avoid shooting yourself in the foot. It's a lot like investing in a new wardrobe to spruce up your image.

That said, let's go over the specifics of the 12 x 12 x 12 rule and how you can manage the perception others have of you.

LOOK THE PART BEFORE GOING TO THE EVENT

You'd be surprised how many people fall short in the fundamental area of appearance. If it's a chamber of commerce networking breakfast, don't go casual, wear a good suit or outfit. You need to be well rested and clearheaded when attending a morning networking session; make a conscious effort to get plenty of sleep the night before. If you're not a morning person, hit the sack earlier than usual so you don't look like the walking dead. Regardless of how many cups of coffee you've had, people can tell if you're not all there.

MAKE SURE YOUR BODY LANGUAGE SENDS THE RIGHT MESSAGE

When it comes to forming networking relationships, most of the important information—trustworthiness, friendliness, sincerity, openness—is communicated through nonverbal cues such as posture, facial expression, and hand gestures. When engaging in conversation, look the other person directly in the eye and stay focused on what he's saying. (With a lot of hustle and bustle going on, this can be harder than it sounds.) Lean a bit into the conversation rather than away from it; don't stand rigid with your arms crossed.

GET YOUR ACT TOGETHER

Make sure you know which pocket your business cards are in, and have plenty on hand. Nothing screams, "One of these days I've got to get organized!" louder than handing a potential referral partner someone else's card.

One more thing: remember to smile when meeting someone for the first time. Studies have shown that if you smile when you talk, you seem more open and forthright. Obviously you don't

BRIAN

At one event a few years ago a man handed me every business card he had but his own. He looked in his left pocket, his right pocket, his coat pocket, and everywhere else, but all he could come up with was other people's business cards. (There were other people waiting for his card as well.) I began to feel sorry for him; you could see his credibility dropping like a stone. Unfortunately, every networking event has someone like that, and believe me, you don't want to be that person.

want to go overboard with this and start grinning and shaking hands like a hyperactive clown; just show that you're having a good time, and that will send the right message.

HAVE THE FIRST 12 WORDS READY TO ROLL OFF YOUR TONGUE

When someone asks you what you do, make sure you're ready with a response that is succinct but memorable. The attention span of the average adult is 20 seconds; a long, drawn-out answer to the question isn't going to work.

We advise our clients to create a *unique selling proposition* (USP), or a mini commercial, that they can readily use while networking (see Chapter 15). We think of ours as our personal answer to the age-old "Whattaya do?" question, which we've personally been asked about a million and a half times.

Here's an example. When someone asks what you do, don't reply with a bland, general statement such as "I'm a consultant." Half the world could say that, and it doesn't tell anybody anything. Instead, you could say, "I work with small to medium-size businesses to help them attract more clients than they could possibly handle." This is short, powerful, and informative.

A USP is obviously something you'll have to tailor to your specific business, but can you see how it packs more punch than just telling people you're a consultant? Whatever 12 or 20 words you choose, make sure your answer is quick and informative without sounding overrehearsed or contrived.

Perception is reality when it comes to meeting people for the first time. If people perceive you as not being right for them, they simply won't be inclined to refer business to you, regardless of the work you can actually do. However, by keeping the 12 x 12 x 12 rule in mind, you'll go a long way toward creating the right impression in the blink of an eye.

13

Where's Your Attention Focused?

Have you ever wondered why most people are better at talking than listening? Or how sometimes when you're talking with someone you can tell that he's only half listening to what you're saying?

Well, if you hope and expect to get more business while networking, then pay special attention to the fact that effective professional networkers have mastered the skill of listening.

DAVID

A client once called me with some questions and concerns. I listened for what seemed like hours but couldn't get a word in edgewise. Finally he asked for advice, which I gladly gave him, specifically and concisely. A few days later I got a thank-you card from him saying what a brilliant conversationalist I was. I still get a kick out of it. By the way, that person is a client to this day, probably because I have two ears and one mouth and use them proportionately.

Fact: The human brain can think at 400 to 450 words per minute; the average person, however, speaks 100 to 150 wpm.

Let's say you're at a networking event, and you're in a conversation with someone who speaks rapidly—maybe somewhere in the neighborhood of 150 wpm. While that person is talking, your brain is processing at a rate of 400 wpm. So, if you're thinking at 400 and the person you're talking to is speaking at 150, then what you do with that extra 250 wpm capacity is going to determine how good a listener you are.

Focused attention means concentrating 100 percent of your attention on the message the other person is communicating.

Where is your attention focused? Are you planning your response while the other person is talking, or are you considering her point and taking mental notes? Are you scanning the room, trying to find the next person to meet, or are you devoting your full attention to this individual?

The reason some people aren't very good listeners is because during most conversations they're spending that extra thinking capacity on something other than the conversation at hand. And in today's e-mail-typing, pager-answering, voice mail-checking world, where multitasking is very much standard operating procedure, everyone seems to be doing two or three things at once.

Recommendation: At your next networking event, shut down your multitasker. Make it a point to block out everyone else in the room and focus your attention on the discussion at hand.

You might argue that not every person you meet will be an immediate prospect for your business. Yes, time is money, and conventional wisdom tells us that you shouldn't be wasting your time with just one person. But here's the thing: even if the one person you're devoting attention to isn't an immediate prospect, you never know whom he might know (Referral! Referral!).

In any event, the last thing you want to do when networking is to seem preoccupied with finding a more important person to talk to. If you've ever been on the other side of that conversation, engaged with someone whose gaze, you began to realize, was focused somewhere over your shoulder like a searchlight, you'll know what we mean when we say that a good swift referral was not the first thing you were thinking about giving that person.

Here's how to avoid being that searchlight networker: Before each event, think of a few questions you'd like to ask each new contact—just two or three questions that will get the other person talking about a subject that might be of interest you. For instance, most of us are interested in hearing how people get new business. Not only can asking questions provide some fresh, new ideas that we might use, but it also creates an opportunity to add value to the conversation by bringing up a point the other person might not have considered. If you're a PR consultant, you might want to ask how your new contact leverages local print and radio media to get more exposure for her business. It's an area you presumably know a lot about, and talking about it gives you an opportunity to gain credibility. If you play your cards right, this person might even turn out to be someone who ultimately contracts your services. However, that will happen only if you take the time to listen closely and understand. Focused attention is essential to doing that.

A friend of ours told us about a person who went a step further and actually used focused attention all the time, not just during networking events. Whenever someone walked into his office, he physically cleared whatever documents he had on his desk and focused all his attention on that person. No cell phones ringing, no emails popping up—just him and that other person. Wow! Now that sends a powerful message.

Imagine being able to send that message to everyone in your professional life. How much of an impact would that have on your ability to get more referrals?

14

Standout Questions

Advance bonus question: What's the easiest way to be seen as a bore?

That's right. Talk about yourself.

So why would anyone think that successful networking means cornering as many people as possible and telling them all about your business? To the contrary, the best way to entertain a new contact and potential future referral partner is to get him to talk about himself and his business.

Your goal in a networking event is to make yourself memorable without talking about yourself. Sounds paradoxical, doesn't it? But if you know how to do it, you will stand out in people's minds when they look back on the event. The secret is simply to ask people questions about themselves and their businesses.

A lot of people you run into at networking events are so busy talking about themselves, their products, and all the great things they can do for you that they never take a breath and ask about you. (These are often the same people who say networking doesn't work for them.) Instead of competing with these folks by getting into a boasting contest about who does the most business, imagine the result of asking questions that encourage them to freely share that information. Now, instead of them talking and you interrupting (or vice versa), you are creating a networking environment in which they're talking, you're listening, and everyone is feeling heard. Not only will this technique help you stand out from the crowd, but it will get you a ton of referrals.

People refer business to people they like and respect. This is why, when you give others time to tell their story and explain their business, your stock automatically rises in their eyes. Throw in the fact that you've got a top-flight product or service—don't worry, eventually the other guy will wind down and you'll get to talk about yourself—and you'll see how it's a lot easier than many people think to create a solid referral partner.

QUESTION TIME

It all begins with your first conversation. If you lead off by asking the right questions—questions that demonstrate a genuine interest in the other person's business—you cultivate an attitude of trust and rapport from the start. By "right questions," we do *not* mean prospecting or qualifying questions, the kind you would ask if you were trying to size up the other person's potential for helping you or to grab some business right off the bat. Those should never be the goal of the first conversation.

Following are five good questions to ask that will make you a standout.

"What Do You Like Best about What You Do?"

If you've been out networking before, you already know that "What do you do?" is one of the first questions people ask you. This isn't necessarily a bad thing, but it doesn't leave you much room to maneuver after both you and your fellow networker have answered the question for each other:

"So what do you do?"

"I'm a public relations consultant. How about you?"

"I see. Well, I own a print shop."

(Awkward four-second pause that seems to go on forever.)

Look how much better it works if you follow up with our question:

"Oh, a print shop. That's interesting. What do you like best about the printing business?"

This leads to more interesting conversation about the other person's business, his likes and dislikes, his experience, and so forth. It makes the conversation flow and lets you relax while you learn about his trade or profession.

What's more, if he's like most of us, he will eventually decide he's talked enough and will ask you the same question—what do you like best about *your* business? Be ready with a good response:

Well, to be honest with you, I really enjoy helping clients get the word out about their business in ways they might not have thought about. Often when people hear "public relations," their first thought is of a big Madison Avenue office—and huge retainer fees.

But that's not how we operate. We help business professionals get more business through print and radio media without it costing them an arm and a leg. I can't tell you how satisfying that is.

A response like this answers the question, raises some important issues, and explains how you're different from others in the industry. If the other person is thinking about using a PR firm or knows someone else who might need one, then you've gone a long way toward setting the stage for a possible referral.

"You Mentioned that You Were in [Industry]. What Got You Started in that Direction?"

This question is much like the previous one in that it gives the other person a chance to talk about personal goals and desires and to look favorably on you for asking it. It also gives you insight into how dedicated she is to her profession and how proficient she may be at it. When you learn what her previous experience has been, you will begin to see ways that you might refer other people to her for specialized products or services.

"Where Else Do You Usually Network?"

Amy Windham, a colleague of Brian's in Atlanta, first brought this one to our attention, and it's an absolute gem. Not only does it help break the ice during that sometimes awkward period just after you've introduced yourself, but it also gives you a chance to talk about something you both know a little bit about.

Another reason we like this question is because it gives you the opportunity to make an instant connection. How? It provides the other person valuable information he didn't previously have, on a topic that's relevant to him. As we all know, a great step toward creating a solid referral partner is to first make a connection with that person.

This is an example of why we believe asking the right questions makes you stand out from the crowd. It started with "Where else do you normally network?" and that dovetailed into an extended conversation about *the other person's* business. Within the

BRIAN

I was at a networking event one morning when I asked a gentleman where else he usually networked. He said that he didn't know of any other networking events around town, since he had just moved to Atlanta.

As a person who likes to consider himself a connoisseur of local networking events, that was music to my ears. I asked him what kind of prospects he was trying to meet—large corporations, small businesses, or something in between. I wanted to get a feel for the types of events that might work for him.

The man replied that his business focused on the technology sector and that he would love to meet anyone in that field. I assured him that this would not be a problem and mentioned the names of a couple of groups I thought could help. You could see the relief in his eyes. He was genuinely grateful that someone was willing to help him out with some business-generating information.

first few minutes, Brian was listening with interest and thinking of ways he could help. This is all you can ask for when meeting someone for the first time.

"What Are Some of Your Biggest Challenges?"

This is a great question that can be used toward the end of the conversation. Of the four questions we've talked about, this usually elicits the longest response. Why? Because you're asking about her reasons, her passion, and her motivation for being in her specific business in the first place. We've had people tell us all sorts of things when we've asked this question.

"How Can I Help You?"

If you've asked a new acquaintance some or all of the previous questions, the conversation has gone well, and you've decided this person is someone you'd like to have in your business network, this is a good question to ask. His answer may tell you something that will enable you to help him, and being helpful is the best way to start building a solid relationship. To a networker who is living the principle of Givers Gain, it's a question that comes naturally, because that networker is one who has adopted the mindset of giving value and service to others without any thought of immediate return. It demonstrates that you have the other person's interests uppermost in your mind, and it's an excellent way to build the credibility and trust you'll want to share with a valuable networking partner.

Remember, everyone has a story. Make it your job to find out what it is.

THE ANSWERS YOU WANT

Asking the right questions is about earning trust and gaining rapport with your new contact. It's about your contact feeling comfortable telling you about her business without competing with you for airtime. But most of all, asking the right questions is about developing a relationship with a future referral partner, so she'll be more than happy to give you any referral that might come her way.

15

Telling Your Company's Story

It's not all about the other person, you know. After you've asked your new acquaintance all the right questions and laid the foundation for a cordial business relationship, the conversation will eventually turn to you, and with any luck you'll find yourself answering many of the same questions you just asked. This is an important part of the give-and-take, and you should be prepared for it. After all, others have to know your business if you're going to get any.

There are two kinds of audiences that need to hear your company's story. One is the people you interact with directly while networking. These could be people you meet and exchange pleasantries with at a chamber of commerce mixer or, more to the point for a networking pro, one or more people in a dedicated referral networking group such as BNI; these are the folks you hope to turn into reliable sources of referrals. The other audience is people you don't meet, at least not right away, but who are told about you by your networking partner or referral source; they are your prospective customers.

YOUR UNIQUE SELLING PROPOSITION

One of the biggest mental hurdles businesspeople have is the idea that word-of-mouth marketing is about telling everyone they see everything they do, and that getting more referrals is simply a matter of talking to more people. But that's not the case at all. In getting your message across, less is more. The trick is to come up with a succinct, memorable unique selling proposition (USP) that you can use at all your networking events.

Your USP is basically a brief description of the purpose of your business, stated in the most succinct and compelling way possible in order to get others to understand the unique value of what you do. A good USP simply tells people what you do, in a manner that gets them to ask how you do it:

- "We work with business owners to help them handle the two biggest challenges they face on a day-to-day basis." —Mike Miller, commercial insurance agent
- "I help busy entrepreneurs market their business in less than 90 days." —Brian Hilliard, sales and marketing coach
- "I help nonprofit organizations connect with their community through the game of golf." —John Parker, golf fundraising specialist
- "I help people network like a pro by teaching them highly effective referral systems." —David Alexander, Chief Networking Officer, Referrals 4 Life

- "I work with municipalities on capital improvement projects in the areas of water, wastewater, and drainage." —Sharmaine James, project engineer in New Orleans
- "I work with bright, successful, family-oriented business owners who are so busy on the immediate that they lose sight of the fundamentals that can affect their family's financial well-being." —Andrew Rodgers, financial advisor
- "I help business owners answer the three most important questions as it relates to their family and the preservation of their business." —Victor Banks, financial advisor
- "I teach people how to create Referrals for Life®." —Ivan Misner, Ph.D., founder of BNI and the Referral Institute

Notice that these USPs are short, sweet, and straight to the point. Your USP tells people the type of client you work with and the benefit you provide. If you meet someone while networking who fits your target market, then her next question should be "How do you do that?" And off you'll go talking about your business.

This is why having a good USP is important. It describes your business in terms of the needs it can fill and allows people to decide whether they want to learn more. Instead of requiring you to identify and approach target markets, it lets your target market self-select.

Let's say you're the proprietor of a preschool day-care center. At a local networking event you meet a man who is single. What's the likelihood he's going to want to hear your message? Slim to none. It has nothing to do with you; it's just that he's not a candidate for your services, so why waste your time and effort on him?

But then suppose this man is recently divorced and, unbeknownst to you, has custody of his children. He might want to learn more about your business—if you've crafted your USP to catch his interest.

Here's how to create your own USP:

- Focus on two or three profitable target markets for your business—groups of people for whom your services are best suited. For the day-care example, one of your target markets might be families with children ages one to five, who live within 15 miles of your business.

- Identify some challenges facing your target market. If you own a restaurant that caters to tourists, one of their likely concerns is finding a good meal at a good price. While traveling, you've probably asked a desk clerk yourself to recommend a good Chinese or Italian restaurant. As a restaurateur, you can address this challenge by getting to know all the hotel staff within five to seven miles of your establishment. Chat with them, bring them some samples, and put together a menu and free-appetizer coupons that they can hand out to arriving guests. If they know you've got the goods, they'll recommend you with confidence.

- Create a snappy one- or two-sentence USP: "I help [target market] [solve problem]." As you saw from the previous examples, that's pretty much the format we used.

Don't confuse a USP with a memory hook. There are some similarities, but a memory hook has a distinctive twist to it that makes it linger in the listener's mind like a catchy melody. If you are in a strong-contact networking group, you know that a memory hook is best used during your 60-second chapter presentation as way of getting members of the group to remember who you are and what products or services you provide.

A memory hook is short and catchy, often using rhyme or wordplay. Here's an example, a great memory hook used by a dentist in California: "I believe in the tooth, the whole tooth, and nothing but the tooth, so help me God." Used to kick off or wrap up a presentation to a large group, it's great at helping people remember who he is and what he does. However, most people would probably edge away from him if he used his memory hook face-to-face at a networking event:

> *Prospect*: "So, what do you do?"
> *Stan*: "I believe in the tooth, the whole tooth . . ."
> *Prospect* (backing away slowly): "Ohh-kaaay . . . ."

See how off that sounds? It just doesn't fit this situation. For a one-to-one conversation, a USP is better:

> "I operate a dental practice. We specialize in prosthetic dentistry."

So if you're in a strong-contact networking group and have a memory hook but no USP, work on developing a good USP. If you have neither, you should start working on both. A memory hook is great on brochures, websites, fliers—even the back of your business card. Think of it as a tagline about your business that gets people to sit up and take notice.

Many people use their memory hooks week after week in a referral group. This is not only annoying but a waste of time. The USP is much more important in this setting. Your goal is to educate your referral partners, and a memory hook just won't do it. Use your memory hook only with groups of people who don't know you.

Regardless of your situation, developing a strong USP that your target market can quickly identify with will put you in great shape for attracting more referrals than you might think possible.

BRIEFING YOUR MESSENGER

When others tell your story, do they get it right? That is, when your CPA friend Clara recommends your business to a potential client, does she know exactly what you do and can she describe it accurately to the prospect?

In his book *From Selling to Serving*, Lou Cassara writes about how important it is to be clear about your purpose (using his term *PVS* in place of our *USP*):

Your PVS (Personal Value Statement) provides the opportunity for your clients, staff, and family to market you effectively. You can build a distribution channel of people who can effectively communicate your value.

Telling your company's story starts at your doorstep. You have to communicate what you do in a way that's clear to your referral sources. This is central to the referral marketing process for any networker because it teaches people how to send you referrals. People must know exactly what you do, what product or service you provide, how well you do it, and in what ways you're better at it than your competitors. You're responsible for communicating this information to your referral sources, and to communicate effectively, you must know your information inside and out.

It may seem like a no-brainer—don't we all know what we do for a living? Of course you do, but can you communicate it clearly and simply to your potential sources? If you think about it, you may find that you're not quite as clear as you thought you were. And if you can't tell your referral sources what you do or what you sell, how can they send you good referrals?

To ensure that your referral marketing campaign is as effective as possible, take a few minutes to get a clear picture of where your business stands today. You may think you know why you're in business, but perhaps it's been years since you've given it serious thought. Now is a good time to reexamine why you're doing what you're doing. Ask yourself the following questions, and write down your answers.

- Why am I in business?
- Why do I do what I do?
- How does my business serve others?

- What do I sell?
- Most important, what are the benefits—not the features—of my product or service?
- Who are my customers?
- What are my target markets? (Be specific; look at all the segments of your business to determine the niche, or niches, you prefer to work with.)
- What are my competencies, and what do I do best?
- How well do I compete?
- How do I stand out from my competition?

Answering these questions will help you tell others what your business is all about, and it will make you more effective at implementing a comprehensive referral program.

After you've written down your answers, think about how you can effectively pass this information to your referral sources.

GETTING SPECIFIC

You're probably so accustomed to the ubiquitous "What do you do?" question at mixers, business events, and seminars that you hardly give a thought to how you're answering that question. It's not enough simply to tell your contacts your job description ("I own and operate a sporting goods store"). To deepen the relationship, you must talk about what you do in a way that, as Cassara says, "communicates the magic of your vision expressed through your words." It should also be specific, should not use jargon, and should be stated in terms of benefits to the customer, not features. Say something along these lines: "I deal in sporting goods, and I specialize in team sports. I've outfitted most of the high school football teams in the district, and I can order custom-fitted shoulder pads and helmets for any player at a deep discount and have it delivered within five days. I also sponsor the local Pop Warner teams."

Too many business professionals and companies try to be all things to all people. Instead, try focusing on the things you do well, and document those things and your vision in a way that you can communicate to others. By clearly understanding what you do, you'll be better able to communicate this to your referral partners, and this will help teach your referral sources whom they can refer to you. Ultimately, that's what networking is all about.

16

Quantity Is Fine, but Quality Is King

One of the biggest misconceptions we've seen about networking is the notion that it's an "all you can eat" affair. In other words, people go to an event, work the room in an effort to meet everyone there, and then judge their success by the number of cards they accumulate. Although we see a certain superficial logic in that, there's one fatal flaw with this kind of thinking: it assumes that the more people you meet at an event, the more successful your networking efforts are—and that's simply not the case.

Businesspeople unfamiliar with referral networking some-times lose track of the fact that networking is the means—not the end—of their business-building activities. They attend three, four, even five events in a week in a desperate grasp for new business. The predictable result is that they stay so busy meeting new people that they never have time to follow up and cultivate those relationships—and how can they expect to get that new business from someone they've only just met? As one of these unfortunates remarked to us, "I feel like I'm always doing business but rarely getting anything done."

BRIAN

A few years back I found myself listening to someone brag about how successful he had been at networking that evening. He had met a bunch of new prospects and had a "stack of cards" right there in his pocket. His unspoken implication was that they just couldn't wait to buy his stuff later on. I was thinking, "OK, but how many of those folks feel that they know you and would be comfortable contracting your services, let alone referring you to their friends?"

I had been watching him "network" all evening. Take my word for it, he wasn't developing relationships. Sure, he shook their hands, told them all about his business, and "listened" for a few seconds. Then, whoosh! He was off to swap cards with the next poor sucker.

If you've ever run into anyone like that, you know that the last thing on your mind was giving him a referral. You simply didn't spend enough time with the guy. And even if you did, you probably didn't like the vibe you got while he was staring over your shoulder, looking at the person he wanted to talk to next.

When you're networking like a pro, you understand the importance of creating a visible identity and asking the right questions. You recognize the value of a unique selling proposition and how the 12 x 12 x 12 rule can manage the perception others have of you. Most important, you realize that meeting people at a networking event is merely the foundation upon which a future business relationship and its referrals are built. It's the *start* of the process—not the beginning, middle, and end of the story, the way our friend was viewing it.

We certainly agree that meeting new people is an integral part of networking, but it's important to remember why we're doing it in the first place: to develop a professional rapport with individuals that will deepen over time into a trusting relationship that will eventually lead to a mutually beneficial and continuous exchange of referrals.

When meeting someone for the first time, focus on the potential relationship you might form. As hard as it may be to suppress your business reflexes, at this stage you cannot make it your goal to sell your services or promote your company. You're there to get to know a new person. A friend of ours told us something his dad always said: "You don't have to sell to friends." That's especially good advice when interacting with new contacts.

This certainly doesn't mean you'll never get to sell anything to people you meet while networking; it does, however, mean that you'll need to employ a different approach. Networking isn't

IVAN

One of my company's directors struck up a conversation with a business owner at a networking function. The business owner told the director, "I'm really good at networking. I've been doing it for a long, long time."

"So what's your secret?" asked our director.

"Well, a friend and I enter a room together," the business owner said. "We draw an imaginary line down the middle. She takes the left side; I take the right. We agree to meet at a certain time to see who has collected the most cards. The loser buys the other one lunch."

The director asked, "So what do you do with all those cards?"

"I enter them into my distribution list and begin to send them information about my services. I have all their information, so that makes them all good prospects, right?"

This is a classic example of an entrepreneur not understanding that networking isn't about simply gathering contact information and following up on it later. That's nothing more than glorified cold calling. It gives me the chills. I used to teach cold calling techniques to businesspeople, and I did it enough to know that I didn't want to ever do it again. I've devoted my entire professional life to teaching the business community that there's a better way to build long-term business.

about closing business or meeting hordes of new people; it's about developing relationships in which future business can be closed. Once you understand that and put it into practice, you'll notice a few things happening to your business.

First, you'll stand out from the crowd with everyone you meet. People often ask us how they can get business at an event when there are so many other people trying to do the same thing. We simply tell them to stand out from the crowd by doing things a bit different. A good way to do that is by asking a new contact good questions and taking the time to listen to her answers. (A good question is one that gets the person talking about herself while helping you understand her business. It is *not* an opportunity for you to vet this person as a client.)

Good questions not only get the ball rolling but take the pressure off you to carry the conversation; meeting new people can be hard enough without feeling you have to be the life of the party to do it. If you're not sure what kinds of questions to ask, go back and re-read Chapter 14, where we talk about them in more detail.

Another good reason for adopting this advanced networking approach is that it will differentiate you from the competition. This is especially vital for mortgage brokers, real estate agents, insurance agents, CPAs, financial planners, and others in highly competitive industries. You can't go to a networking event without running into at least one person in some of those fields.

When you're networking like a pro and treating new contacts as future referral partners, you'll absolutely blow away any competitors who will still feel compelled to meet as many people as they can. Why? Because when you call your contacts back, they'll actually remember who you are and will be willing to meet with you again. This is obviously a critical next step for securing more business.

With all of that in mind, let's take a look at some specific steps you can take toward getting more business from your very next event.

- *Limit the number of contacts per event.* The most important thing is the quality of the contacts, which means the type of contact, the relevance to your business and interests, how good a connection you're making, and the individual involved. At a typical event, five to ten might be all you can handle. This may not seem like a lot of contacts, but it's really more than enough when you're talking to the right people. (That's why it's so important to have a network strategy, which we covered in Part II.) If you attend two events per week, that's 8 (or more) events a month, or 40 to 80 new contacts every 30 days. Continue to do that over the next couple of months—while following up with the people that you've met—and you'll soon have more than enough high-quality contacts to keep you busy.

- *Spend five to ten minutes talking and listening to each person.* Just because you're not handing out your business card to 1,001 people doesn't mean you should spend 20 minutes talking to just one individual. Invest a few minutes in getting to know each person. Make sure to ask for her business card. Then follow up with her after the event; this is where the heavy lifting takes place. Remember, all we're doing now is setting the stage for future business.

- *Write notes on the backs of people's cards.* Not only will writing notes help you remember what the other person said at an event, but it will slow you down a bit so you won't be running around trying to meet the next person. On the front of the card you can write the date and name of the event where you met the person; on the back, a few quick notes about the conversation or anything else of note. When you contact the person later, this will give you something to refer to.

Here are a few things to remember when it comes to meeting new people:

IVAN

CAUTION! In some cultures, especially some Asian countries, people will take great offense if you write on their business cards. If you are in doubt, ask the person if it's all right: "Do you mind if I make a note on the back of your card to remind me to get back to you on that?" This will allow her to give you permission, if she wishes, and it demonstrates that you are interested in responding to her questions or comments. Then be absolutely sure you do respond; don't let it slide.

· You're not interested in selling anything to the person you're just meeting; you want to find some way you can help her. You understand, of course, that what goes around comes around, usually in the form of referrals for your business.

· You want to create a visible identity with everyone you meet. A visible identity is the answer to this question: "How can I differentiate myself, in the mind of this other person, from the other five people she's already met?"

Keeping those two ideas in mind will give you a leg up when meeting new contacts. Using this simple, Givers Gain approach, you'll see an uptick in the amount of new business and referrals you get while networking.

PART IV

MAKING YOUR NETWORK WORK

17

How Deep Is Your Network?

In Southern California, there are many tall, lush eucalyptus trees that topple over fairly easily in strong winds. Every year, some are uprooted and blown over, and you can then see that their root system is broad but not at all deep. Trees with deep taproots, such as pecan and mesquite, are less vulnerable.

To be strong and resilient, your network should be like a deep-rooted tree. Sure, when you're first growing your network, you're interested in making it broader so it will have more connections, but when it comes to making it work for you, your network needs to have depth as well as breadth.

When you're considering asking someone in your personal network for a favor, ask yourself if she's a contact or a connection. A contact is someone you know, but with whom you haven't fully established a strong relationship; a connection is someone who knows you and trusts you because you've taken the time to establish credibility with her. Among the most important connections you can make are those with your referral sources, with prospects these referral sources bring you, and with customers you recruit from the prospects.

You may have a lot of contacts, but how well do you know them, and how well do they know you? It's unrealistic to expect help from contacts who don't know you well and feel no loyalty to you. If you're spending a lot of time going out and meeting new contacts, think about how much more profitably your time might be spent if you devoted more of it to turning existing contacts into connections.

The more people you know, the broader your network; the better you know them, the deeper. You can't know everybody equally well, of course. Just as some of your friends are closer to you than others, you will have deeper relationships with some of your networking partners than with others. These are the people you know best, people you believe and trust, people to whom you don't hesitate to offer help and referrals whenever you see the opportunity, and they are people you trust and count on to promote your business to their clients, to cross-market your products or services, and to give you high-quality referrals.

BUILDING QUALITY RELATIONSHIPS

How do you make your network deep? By developing and nurturing trusting relationships with a number of your closest networking partners. This is a long-term goal; you need to have a strong, deep network in place well before you can depend on it for the bulk of your business.

Like all of us, you're busier than a cross-eyed Frisbee dog; even so, it will pay off in the end if you use some of your time to deepen your relationships with your referral sources. Go beyond the normal business interactions; get to know them away from work; invite them to backyard barbecues and ball games. The better your friendship, the more you can expect from each other's networking.

There are proven ways to deepen the roots of your network, and most of them hinge on your attitude toward your networking partners. This is where Givers Gain becomes the gold standard for all your actions.

It all comes down to this: focusing on others is the most powerful way of deepening and widening your network. Go into each interaction with one thought uppermost in your mind: What can I do for this person? Do whatever you can to bring business and contacts to your networking partners. Share information with them; invite them to business meetings where they can meet potential clients; be generous with your time, your knowledge, and your referrals. Plant in their minds the idea that whenever you call or show up, good things will swiftly follow.

Any successful relationship, whether personal or business, is unique to every pair of individuals and evolves over time. It starts out tentative, fragile, full of unfulfilled possibilities and expectations. It grows stronger with experience and familiarity. It matures into trust and commitment. As it deepens, it evolves through three phases: visibility, credibility, and profitability. We call this the VCP Process®.

VISIBILITY TO CREDIBILITY TO PROFITABILITY

The VCP Process describes the creation, growth, and strengthening of business, professional, and personal relationships; it is useful for assessing the status of a relationship and where it fits in the process of getting referrals. It can be used to nurture the growth of an effective and rewarding relationship with a prospective friend, client, co-worker, vendor, colleague, or family member. When fully realized, such a relationship is mutually rewarding and thus self-perpetuating.

Visibility

In the first phase of growing a relationship, you and another individual become aware of each other—that is, visible to each other. In business terms, a potential source of referrals or a potential customer becomes aware of the nature of your business, perhaps because of your PR and advertising efforts or perhaps through someone you both know. This person may observe you in the act of conducting business or relating with the people around you. The two of you begin to communicate and establish links—perhaps a question or two over the phone about product availability. You may become personally acquainted and work on a first-name basis, but you know little about each other. A combination of many such relationships forms a casual-contact network, a sort of de facto association based on one or more shared interests.

The visibility phase is important because it creates recognition and awareness. The greater your visibility, the more widely known you will be, the more information you will obtain about others, the more opportunities you will be exposed to, and the greater will be your chances of being accepted by other individuals or groups as someone to whom they can or should refer business. Visibility must be actively maintained and developed; without it, you cannot move on to the next level, credibility.

Credibility

Once you and your new acquaintance begin to form expectations of each other and the expectations are fulfilled, your relationship can enter the credibility stage. If each person is confident of gaining satisfaction from the relationship, then it will continue to strengthen.

Credibility is the quality of being reliable, worthy of confidence. Credibility grows when appointments are kept, promises are acted upon, facts are verified, and services are rendered. The old saying that results speak louder than words is true. Failure to live up to expectations—to keep both explicit and implicit promises—can kill a budding relationship before it breaks the surface of the ground and can create visibility of a kind you don't want.

To determine how credible you are, people often turn to third parties. They ask someone they know who has known you longer or perhaps has done business with you. Will that person vouch for you? Are you honest? Are your products and services effective? Are you someone who can be counted on in a crunch?

Profitability

The mature relationship, whether business or personal, can be defined in terms of its profitability. Is it mutually rewarding? Do both partners gain satisfaction from it? Does it maintain itself by providing benefits to both? If it doesn't profit both partners to keep it going, it probably will not endure.

BE PATIENT

The time it takes to pass through the phases of a developing relationship is highly variable. It's not always easy to determine when profitability has been achieved: A week? A month? A year? In a time of urgent need, you and a client may proceed from visibility to credibility overnight. The same is true of profitability; it may happen quickly, or it may take years, but most likely it will be somewhere in between. It will depend on the frequency and quality of the contacts and especially on the desire of both parties to move the relationship forward.

Shortsightedness can impede the full development of the relationship. Perhaps you're a customer who has done business with a certain vendor off and on for several months, but to save pennies you keep hunting around for the lowest price, ignoring the value this vendor provides in terms of service, hours, goodwill, and reliability. Are you really profiting from the relationship, or are you stunting its growth? Perhaps if you gave this vendor all your business, you could work out terms that would benefit both of you. Profitability is not found by bargain hunting. It must be cultivated, and, like farming, it takes patience.

Visibility and credibility are important in the relationship-building stages of the referral marketing process. But when you have established an effective referral generation system, you will have entered the profitability stage of your relationships with many people—the people who send you referrals and the customers you recruit as a result. It's an essential part of successful relationship marketing and networking.

18

Gaining Their Confidence

When it comes to getting referrals from your network, confidence is a vital component—not your confidence, but the confidence your fellow network members have in you. None of them wants to risk her personal reputation by referring business, information, or contacts to a stranger. And even though you may have known many of your fellow networkers for quite some time, until they've gained a certain level of confidence that referring contacts to you will not harm their reputation with their clients, associates, friends, or family, you're still a stranger.

What exactly is this level of confidence? The referral confidence curve shown in Figure 18.1 illustrates the dynamics of the process. Your success in getting referrals depends partly on your competence, of course, but more on how far up the confidence curve the referrer's confidence in you has progressed. If you're at point B in the relationship, you've known each other for a while but you still haven't quite achieved the necessary confidence level with this person to get a referral from her. When you reach point C, she'll feel comfortable recommending you to friends.

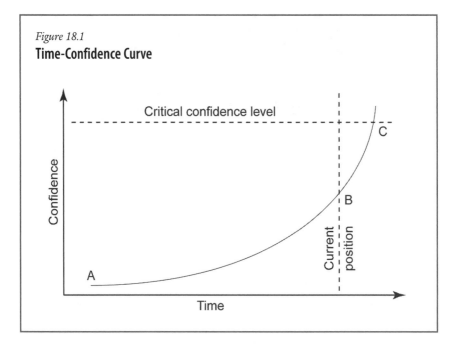

Figure 18.1
Time-Confidence Curve

The shape of the curve shows why planning referral-based marketing means cultivating long-term relationships. Confidence grows slowly at first, then more quickly as the relationship matures. The level of confidence required reflects the level of risk perceived by the referrer.

GETTING THERE

How long will it take you to reach the critical level of confidence with your networking friends? Aside from the quality of your products or services, this depends on four main factors.

1. Your Profession

The more significant the business being referred, the greater the risk to the referrer's reputation. If you're a florist, it may take only a week or two for people who try your services to recommend you on the basis of their experience with you. The risk associated with referring a florist is usually small, unless you're bidding on a large corporate account that also may be your referrer's top client. If you're a lawyer, accountant, or investment advisor, it may take you six months or a year to reach the critical confidence level. However, since the stakes are higher, your referrer stands to gain more if the results are successful (see Figure 18.2). She will

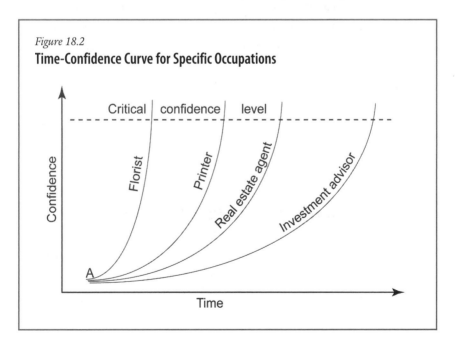

Figure 18.2
Time-Confidence Curve for Specific Occupations

enhance her reputation as someone who knows the right people to get things done.

No matter what line of work you're in, if you don't perform well, your referrer will learn of it and your progress on the confidence curve will drop back to zero. You may not get another referral from that source, but if you do, it will take longer the second time. Third time? Don't ask.

2. How Well You Educate Others about Your Business

Don't assume that your fellow networkers understand your company or industry well enough to refer you confidently. Most have enough of a job keeping up with their own business and personal concerns. You have to educate them and keep on educating them as long as you're in business. The best way is to speak to large, receptive groups; a networking group is ideal, because everybody is expected to address the group at regular intervals. Make your presentation interesting and stimulating. Tell them how your product or service improves business or life. Tell them who, what, when, where, and how. Each time you speak, present a new aspect of your business. Let your knowledge and eloquence persuade them that you are very good at what you do. They will grow confident that you cannot seriously injure their reputations with their contacts, and your name will come to mind whenever a referral opportunity arises.

3. The Help You Give Others in Moving Up Their Own Referral Confidence Curves

If you can endorse the quality of products or services offered by a networking partner—that is, increase others' confidence in him—your partner will be disposed to return the favor. Testimonials from one or two of your partners may, in turn, trigger a much larger and more valuable referral from another partner who was waiting for more evidence before taking a risk on you.

4. The Time You Invest in Learning about Others' Businesses

If you want someone to learn about the value of your products or services, you have to spend time learning about the value of his. The best way to do this is one-on-one: "John, I'd like to be able to refer more business to you, but I need a deeper understanding of what your company does and how you operate. Could we get together one day next week to discuss this?" Although you don't say so, John understands that he will learn something more about your business at the same time. Serious master networkers meet regularly to raise each other's understanding of their businesses.

STAYING FOR THE LONG HAUL

It's not always easy to know how far you've progressed up your confidence curve. Many networkers spend a lot of time and effort trying to build others' confidence in them, then, on the brink of success, grow discouraged and stop attending meetings. (In terms of the first graph on page 132, they work hard long enough to get from point A to point B, then quit, never realizing how close they are to point C.) How would you feel if someone found you a terrific referral about two weeks after you dropped out of sight?

Here's what you can do to gain perspective on your efforts and the results they are producing. Ask yourself the following four questions, and keep asking them over and over until you have attained success and the answers become obvious.

1. Am I being realistic about the time it will take, in my profession, to gain the critical level of confidence?

2. Am I regularly making stimulating, educational presentations to my fellow networkers about the value I provide to my clients?

3. Am I doing business with others in my group so I can give them dynamic testimonials and steer business to them in hopes they will return the favor?

4. Am I meeting regularly with my networking colleagues to learn about their businesses so I can confidently refer my contacts to them?

If you're following these simple tactics, then you are well along the road to getting all the referrals from others' networks that you deserve.

(This material was adapted from an article by Martin Lawson in *Masters of Networking*, by Ivan Misner and Don Morgan.)

19

Leveraging New Contacts

We go to networking events to meet new people and generate interest in our firm. Meeting people is an essential part of the networking process. If you're just getting started, it's where you'll spend most of your networking time, but even in a mature network, you'll devote some of your time to adding new contacts to your network—people who can help your business, put you in touch with other people they know, or simply provide valuable information.

But for a true networker, meeting people is only the first step in a long, continuing process.

Ultimately, your objective as a networker is to have a broad network of contacts that you can call on to help you solve problems and rustle up new business. If you intend to achieve that objective consistently, reliably, and profitably for as long as your business lasts, many of your relationships will have to be deep, trusting, mutually beneficial associations.

At the event itself, it's tough to have a conversation that lasts longer than a couple of minutes. That's why you should never expect to do much business at a networking event, especially with people you've just met. Nevertheless, you don't have to wait until your relationships are mature in order to begin discovering business opportunities for your new contacts and yourself. In fact, it's often a good way to kick-start a new relationship.

The secret is in the follow-through.

GETTING TO THE NEXT STAGE

How can you move a relationship with someone you just met to the point where she feels comfortable passing you a referral? It depends in part on how you came into contact with her in the first place. Let's say you did so while giving a brief presentation to a group of people who are in your target market. Assuming you did a good job, then you absolutely have the possibility of receiving a referral, even though you just met. Why? Because the presentation moved you from visibility to credibility in her mind (Chapter 17), and now she's probably willing to risk her reputation and recommend you to someone she knows.

The same thing is true when you're out networking. If you have a good conversation with someone and truly add value to the conversation, then moving from visibility to credibility isn't that difficult, and you'll be in great shape for getting some referral-based business. What's more, it's not terribly important whether the person is someone you might do business with directly. Even if your businesses don't match up, the other person might have information that's useful or might know other people you'd like to get in contact with. It's often worthwhile developing a networking relationship with people who have little in common with you, because they can bring an entirely new network into contact with yours and broaden your business horizons.

Just bear in mind that even if there is a strong possibility that you're going to do business with this new contact, it's probably not going to happen there at the networking event, where conversations last anywhere from an eye-blink three minutes to a long-winded seven. Instant business is not likely to be had. But if you follow up with a quick note a few days later, you can make some one-to-one time and come up with ways the two of you can help each other. That meeting is where you'll have your best opportunity for a quick referral.

SORTING OUT WHO'S WHO

Here's how the process can work.

The first order of business, after you've met a lot of new people and come home with a pocketful of business cards, is to perform a little triage. You need to separate the people you think might become new clients or referral partners *right now* from the ones who might be valuable contacts sometime in the future but not right away. Let's call the first group your A list, the rest your B list. (Sounds kind of Hollywood, doesn't it?) When you enter them into your database, this would be one good criterion to include (along with type of business, address, phone number, event where you met, and others).

Now that you've got your contacts filed away neatly, take a look first at your B list. You want these folks to know you enjoyed meeting them, and you want to keep the door open for doing business with them later on if a good opportunity arises. You can do this with a quick note by either e-mail or snail mail:

Jim—

My name is John Smith, and I'm the consultant who met you the other day over at the chamber. I just wanted to say that I really enjoyed our conversation—and it sounds like you're really doing well and staying busy.

Anyway, it was good talking to you, and if I can help you out in any way, please let me know.

John

See how easy that was? If you find you need to reconnect with this person at some later time, you'll at least have some traction in the relationship simply because you followed up with a quick e-mail.

Now, what about your A list? These are people who have immediate potential as referral partners. You need to follow up quickly—within a few days, before you drop off their radars.

First, initiate a "coffee connection" with each of your new contacts, a follow-up meeting where you can get to know her and find out how you can help her. That's right—you're going to offer help. Anything short of trying to find ways to help her will generally be treated as a sales call instead of a relationship-building contact. To ask for this first meeting, either a handwritten note or an e-mail is acceptable.

Handwritten notes are traditional, but they're going the way of the dinosaur in today's instant-messaging, thumbs-on-a-BlackBerry world, which of course means that writing your invitation on paper will make you stand out from the crowd. On the other hand, who has time to buy a card, find a stamp, look up the address, fill the inkwell, pluck an ostrich plume, and scratch out the message? Not us. We go with e-mail, which is fast, easy, efficient, and perfectly acceptable if it doesn't get caught in a spam

IVAN

All things being equal, a handwritten note is tradition-ally considered the best way to follow up. The problem is that I just don't do it consistently. Is it really the best method if you know you're not going to do it reliably? I don't think so. That's why I prefer to follow up with an e-mail message, a phone call, or better yet, a card (using something like the SendOutCards system, at SendOutCards.com, an easy, convenient online service). Those are the things I'm in the habit of doing, and I'm most likely to follow up in a timely way if I stick to what I do best.

filter (but keep an eye on your spelling). The best approach is whatever one you can commit to using consistently.

Whether you settle on using paper or electrons, you'll want to send out a note along the following lines a day or two after the event.

Subject: Nice to Meet You—Chamber Event (1/23)

Jim—

My name is Jane Smith, and I'm the consultant who met you the other day at the chamber event. Hey listen, I just wanted to say I really enjoyed our conversation and was hoping I could learn a little bit more about what you do.

I'm thinking we can get together for a quick cup of coffee. That way, if I run into someone who could use your services, I can point him in your direction.

I'm pretty booked this week, but how does next Tuesday morning sound for something over at Starbucks?

Again, great talking to you, and if I can help your business in any way, please let me know.

Jane

Let's take a look at this e-mail and see exactly what you're doing. *First, you're reminding the person who you are and where you met.* You do this with the subject line (if sending an e-mail) and the first sentence. You include the date of the event to remind him which meeting you're talking about. This keeps your message from being inadvertently deleted if he doesn't recognize your name immediately.

Second, you're positively acknowledging your conversation and asking to get together so you can learn more about what he does. That way, you point out, if you run into someone who could use *his* services, you can direct that person to your new contact.

You may ask, "What if I meet someone who isn't a potential client and isn't in a field that can refer business to me? Should I follow up with him anyway?" Absolutely! You never know whom other people know; even a quick little "Nice to meet you" e-mail, is better than not doing anything at all and hoping he remembers you later when you discover a need to do business with him.

MAKING THE MOST OF FACE TIME
Warming Up

What do you do when you meet your new contact at the coffee-house? Get there first and pick out a good table. When he arrives, smile, shake hands, and make sure he's seated in a good spot, not in the glare of that car windshield. Chat a bit about small stuff (weather, traffic) to get the conversation started. After a couple of minutes of this, suggest going to the counter to order. As you're standing in line, you can chat about your coffee preferences or perhaps what you'd recommend.

After coming back to the table, here's what you say: "Now, I remember in our last conversation you said you were a [occupation]. I know we talked a little about it before, but maybe you could fill in the blanks and tell me more about what you do."

That is an absolute can't-miss, knock-it-out-of-the-park opening, guaranteed to get him talking about himself and his business. So far, so good. After he's done with answering the initial volley, here are some good follow-up questions:

- So, how long have you been doing this?
- How did you get into this line of work?
- Where are your favorite places to network?
- How do you go about getting new business?

That last one might seem a little odd, but it's absolutely vital to the meeting. It gets him thinking about the ways new customers come to know about him, including referrals. So, later on in the discussion when you ask for business, either with him or with someone he knows, it won't seem like you're coming out of left field. At this point your contact will probably say that most of his business comes from word-of-mouth.

"Interesting," you say. "Tell me a little bit about your typical client. Do you work mostly with consumers, businesses . . . ?" You're trying to get a feel for his client profile. What does his typical client look like? Does he work primarily with businesses or consumers? Small companies or large? Locally or nationally?

Fork in the Road

Fifteen or 20 minutes into the conversation, you should have a pretty good picture of his ideal client. You now have three choices:

- *Option 1.* If you know someone who can use his services directly, you say, "Well, you know, I have a friend who can really use your services. Would it be okay if I gave her a call and the two of you exchanged information? I think she'd get a lot out of meeting you."

- *Option 2.* If you don't know someone who can use his services directly, don't panic. This happens more often than not, but you can still help him out. Let's say your new contact targets small to midsize technology companies. You might not know of a director who fits that prospect profile, but perhaps you do know of someone who's involved in the National Association of Technology Directors. (There's an association for everything.) You could give your new contact this person's name and offer to try to arrange a meeting or maybe even an opportunity to give a presentation at one of the group's conferences. Even though you might not know of someone directly who could use your contact's services, you might know of someone who could clearly move this person's business forward.

- *Option 3.* If you don't know anyone at all who can help, that's fine, too. Just say, "You know, Jim, I can't think of anyone off the top of my head who could use your services, but if I do, is it all right for me to get back to you?" As long as you show you're genuinely interested in helping him out, your new contact should be pleased with that.

Now, tell your contact what you do and ask for a referral (finally). Yes, it seems we've been talking about how you can help this person a lot more than how you can get new business yourself. And that's absolutely true.

Unfortunately, our society has become so skeptical and distrustful that most people are looking out only for themselves. Even though this person agreed to meet with you for coffee, you need to demonstrate that you have his business interests in mind as well.

How do you do that with someone you just met and who doesn't really know you? By spending the first 25 minutes of the meeting listening to his situation and actively trying to help him get more business. Most people love getting new business but rarely spend time learning about someone else's so they can help out with a referral of their own.

We've been doing this for a long time now, and we've seen again and again that actions speak louder than words. So if you spend some quality time with someone, helping him get more business, that speaks volumes for your sincerity.

Cementing the Connection

Now that you've done all of that, how do you get new business? Give this a try:

"Well, as you know, Jim, I help organizations get the word out about their business through a coordinated word-of-mouth program. So, as you get to know more about me, if you know of a small to medium-size business such as a credit union, insurance company, or community bank that has a sales force looking to generate more word-of-mouth business, that would be a great referral for me."

See how easy that was?

First, you stated what you do and the area you specialize in. This defines your target market.

After that, you asked him to consider you for a referral. Notice how we're not focused on getting business from that person? If it works out that way, great, but our primary objective is to get business from other people he knows.

We're taking a page out of the recruiter's playbook with this one. As anyone who has worked in corporate America knows, when a recruiter calls, it's never to find *you* a job, because she knows, of course, that you're deliriously happy where you are and would never think of leaving. Instead, she describes a position that might dovetail nicely with your career, then asks whether you know "anyone who might be interested," knowing full well, of course, that the first person you think of will be yourself.

You're doing the same thing here with your contact. You're not asking for *his* business, but if he volunteers himself as a possible candidate for your services, you'll certainly welcome it, just as you'll be happy to help anyone he refers to you. At this point, he might ask some questions about you and your business; after all, most of the time so far has been spent talking about his business. Answer calmly and professionally, ideally with a story or two that illustrates how you've helped previous clients. Once he's gotten comfortable with you and you see an opening, feel free to ask for the business again ("If you happen to know someone . . .").

The key is to make the person feel comfortable in putting his name on the line by giving you a referral. *Under no circumstances* is he to feel you're directly asking him for *his* business. That's one of the biggest mistakes most people make, and it will have the exact opposite effect. He also shouldn't feel pressured into making a decision right there. If he doesn't have anyone in mind (which will happen), simply say something like this: "Well, I have an online newsletter that I e-mail to a select list of professionals every two weeks. It talks about marketing and advertising and some different ways to get the word out about your business. Is it all right if I include you on our next distribution?"

If you ask it correctly, 95 percent of the people you have a good conversation with will have no problem saying yes to a question like this. If you don't actually have an electronic newsletter yet, let him know it's in the works. It's never too early to get people's e-mail addresses and start building your database.

20

The Power of Your Database

Here are some numbers that will curl your hair. Did you know that the average businessperson's contact database contains 859 names? Well, it's true, according to a study conducted by AT&T Labs, the New Jersey Institute of Technology, and the University of Minnesota.

Think about that for a minute. Do you have close to a thousand contacts at your fingertips? Can you name a hundred? Fifty?

OK, open all the drawers in your desk where you have tossed the business cards you've accumulated over the last few years. Now does it look more like a thousand? We thought so. And this doesn't even count the hundreds or thousands of people you've shaken hands with, talked with on the phone, or otherwise met without exchanging business cards.

"Not guilty," you say. "I've got a card file right here in front of me that contains hundreds of cards, complete with telephone numbers."

Yes, that's right. And if you're the average, well-organized card filer with 859 contacts, how many of them have you actually contacted in the last year or two? About 20 percent.

So even if you're the typical organized card filer, you haven't been taking advantage of most of the contacts you've made. You haven't followed up, for one reason or another. Maybe you wanted to or intended to but didn't know what to say or how to start. Or maybe you took a look at the pile of cards and decided it was hopeless.

Look, if you're an enterprising businessperson who expects to build your word-of-mouth business, you can't afford to ignore 80 percent of the people you meet. Besides, consider this: If you can harness this untapped resource, you may never again need to make a cold call. Doesn't that give you some incentive? Good.

POWERING UP YOUR DATABASE

The first step is the big one: enter all your contact information in an electronic database. We can hear your screams already, and here's how we answer them:

- *"I don't like computers. I prefer the personal touch."* We like the personal touch, too, but first you have to figure out which of the hundreds of people you've met that you want to approach personally, and when, and how, and why. In the end, it's all personal contact. The database just gives you an orderly way of staying in personal touch with hundreds of contacts, rather than 10 or 20.

- *"My card holder is easier to carry around."* If you can run a thriving business on the names you carry in your pocket, more power to you. You don't need this book; you need to write your own.
- *"Hey, I've got everything in my card file already. I can look up anybody with a few flips of my finger. Why do I need a computer database?"* Well, pull up a chair and we'll explain.

If you're meeting three to five new people each week, and you've been in the business (or plan to be) for more than a year, then you're looking at 150 to 250 new contacts every year. Multiply that by the number of years you plan on being in business, and you'll get an idea as to the volume we're talking about.

Now, put your hands on your card file. What's the name of that CPA you met at the Phoenix conference who liked skydiving and was an expert on sports gear retail? Ready, set, go!

Got it yet? No, your card file doesn't even give you a hint as to where to start looking. But with our computer database, we've already done a quick search and come up with the name.

Yes, you can scribble some code on the corners of your cards, but that's still a slow, primitive, and limited way to search for one needle in a haystack of names. If you've got lots of time on your hands, tons of patience, a boutique business, or total recall, perhaps you can do without an electronic database. Otherwise, you're driving a horse and buggy on a ten-lane freeway.

There are many good database programs available. One that we recommend is Relate2Profit.com, but you can also use Microsoft Outlook, ACT!, or any other database that suits your computer, your work style, and your personal preferences. The important thing is to have the capability to search and sort by many categories—not just name, but type of business, networking event, age, and so on.

One of the reasons we like Relate2Profit.com is that it has integrated the VCP Process (with our permission) into its system (see Chapter 17, "How Deep Is Your Network?"). The database has been set up to allow users to easily identify where they are in the VCP Process with, and communicate the appropriate information to, each contact. Where you are in the relationship should help determine the type and frequency of your touch points with your contacts. For example, you should send different information to people depending on whether you are at visibility or credibility or especially profitability with them.

Any contact database will allow you to enter basic information such as business name, business type, street address, telephone number, e-mail, website, and so forth. What you really want to look for, if you're not using Relate2Profit.com, is a database that is flexible enough to let you add your own sorting categories—criteria that mean something to you but perhaps not to most people who would purchase and use the software. For example, you should be able to set up a field where you can categorize each contact as V, C, or P.

Here are some other custom sorting criteria that you may find useful as a networker:

- Date first met
- Event first met
- Date last contacted
- Last referral sent
- Date last referral sent
- Last referral received
- Date last referral received
- Organization membership or attendance
- Age
- Sex
- Single or married
- Number of children
- Personal interests or hobbies

Using criteria such as these, you can quickly sort out, for example, all the investment bankers you met at chamber mixers within the last six months, or you can find that elusive Mandarin-speaking landscape architect you met at some conference three years ago but whose name or city you can't remember. You can print out a list of names, addresses, and telephone numbers of new contacts you have made in the last two months but haven't followed up with. And you can quickly list all networking associates who have given you referrals within the past six months but have received none from you for at least three.

There's one other category that you might want to include in your database sorting criteria. Is the contact an A contact (someone you think might become a new client or referral partner right away) or a B (someone you'd like to consider further down the line)? (See Chapter 19, "Leveraging New Contacts.") We explain the reason for this a bit later.

PUTTING YOUR DATABASE TO WORK

Once you've got all your contacts entered and the relevant data in the correct fields, you can begin to create the magic that a good electronic database puts at your fingertips. There are as many ways to use a database for networking as there are networkers, but we discuss here a couple of ways your database can become a powerful tool in your networking activities.

First, let's say you want to want to organize your newest contacts and identify a number of them you think are most likely to become valued networking partners. You can start by sorting your database into the three categories we've already talked about: V, C, and P.

Those in the P (profitability) group are contacts you've already established a profitable relationship with, through either direct business dealings or referrals. This group probably includes your oldest and closest associates. You can set these aside for now.

The C (credibility) group are people you know well enough to be confident in their ability and integrity, and who in turn are confident in yours. You haven't necessarily done business with them, but you've established a good relationship and are prepared to swap referrals when the opportunity arises. Set these aside as well.

It's the V (visibility) group you're interested in today. These are people you've met but don't yet know much about, other than what business they're in. They know who you are and perhaps a few facts about your business. Some you've met recently, others a while back. You haven't sat down and had a good face-to-face discussion with any of them. They are people with unknown potential for your network.

Now it's time to sort the V records—that is, to break this group down into other subgroups. You've identified each contact as an A-list contact or a B-list contact, right? We described these categories in Chapter 19, "Leveraging New Contacts." Your A list includes people you believe to have immediate potential as referral partners.

Once you've produced your A list, sort it next by date—say, contacts from this week and contacts from more than a week ago. As we recommended earlier, you should try to arrange a coffee connection as soon as possible with the most recent contacts. For those you've let go more than a week or two, start your e-mail with a quick introduction and an apology for not contacting them sooner ("I meant to catch up with you earlier, but things got really busy here after the conference"), then go straight into an invitation for coffee.

Now, what about your B list, the ones left over after you've sorted out the A contacts? As described in Chapter 19, write the recent ones a nice follow-up letter in case you change your mind and decide to get together with them later. B contacts that are more than a few weeks old are best forgotten, since they didn't warrant a face-to-face with you in the first place; a follow-up note weeks after the event probably won't cut it. File them away and promise yourself you'll be more diligent next time.

This is only one of many ways to use your automated database. Another good idea is to sort out a list of credibility contacts and try to meet at least one of them each week. If it hasn't been too long since your last meeting, a quick e-mail or phone call might be enough to suggest a coffee break or lunch where you can ask how things are going and let him know what's new with you. If it's been longer than a few months, however, a phone call might seem to be coming out of left field. An e-mail like the following might be more appropriate:

Jim—

This is Sally. We met at the Greater Heights chamber a few months ago. How are you?

Hey listen, things have been super busy over here so I apologize for not contacting you earlier, but I just wanted to touch base and see what your calendar looked like over the next couple of weeks.

As you know I meet many different people and would like to learn more about what you do, so if I meet someone who could use your services, I can point him or her in your direction.

I was thinking about a quick cup of coffee or something, 20 to 30 minutes max. So just let me know what dates work best for you.

I look forward to keeping in touch. Talk to you soon.

Sally Sue

That should be good enough for 40 or 50 percent of your contacts to respond, and you'll be off and running.

The third way to make your database work for you is through an online newsletter. Newsletters are great ways to stay in front of people you meet when networking, while simultaneously enhancing your credibility . . . if it's done correctly. In other words, a monthly "update" to your database about your latest sale items is not our idea of enhancing creditability.

Eric Groves, senior vice president of global market development at Constant Contact (ConstantContact.com), has four tips for marketing to your folks via e-mail:

1. Build a quality list of people who know and trust you: they're the ones who open your mail.
2. Take the time out of your day to create a strategy for your e-mail. What do you want to have happen when people read your message?
3. Execute on your strategy by writing content that's not about you, but shares what you know. People will forward messages that make them seem smart.
4. Ask for feedback and engage your customers in the process. Recognize people who give you insight.

Groves summarizes the secret of great e-zine content: "Be brief, be bright, and be gone."

The bottom line is that while your database may take some work to put together, having ways to put it into action as discussed in this chapter, will go a long way toward your long-term business success.

21

The Referral Process

A lot of what we've said so far emphasizes the circuitous, sometimes mysterious nature of referral networking. In a deep, broad-based, mature referral network, where you spend a lot of time doing good things for others without looking for a direct reward, and where the good that you do winds its way through the system and eventually comes back to you in the form of referrals, it may seem odd to describe referral networking as a system. But that is what it is, and when it comes to the actions of generating, developing, and closing a business deal through a referral, there is a well-defined, systematic process.

What is a referral? It's not as simple as it's sometimes made out to be. We leave college and go into business knowing little about referrals, because referral marketing is rarely part of the curriculum. We know what a great thing it is to get a referral, because it generally means lucrative business with a reliable client. We often think of it simply as a connection to someone we can call on to do business with or, if it's not our kind of business, someone we can refer to someone else.

We understand that referrals are the best kind of business. What we don't understand is how to make them happen when we

DAVID

I do training and consulting on personal referral marketing. When I get a referral, my minimum expectation is that the person providing the referral must know the person he is referring so well that he can set up a meeting between the two of us.

When the meeting has been set, what do you think my chances are of closing that deal? They're very good. Now, if that referral were just a name and some contact information, perhaps with an okay to mention the referrer's name, what would be my chances of even getting an appointment? Right. Not so good.

Make sure your referral partners know the contact well enough to brief you on the best approach, understand what you do well enough to recommend you, and then pass the ball to you. That sets you up for a slam dunk.

want them and, when they come in, how to get the best results from them and make them last.

The referral process is a system that has a lot of feedback built into it. If you follow it for every referral, you will get predictable results: more closed business deals and a never-ending supply of referrals. We have broken it down into eight easy steps.

STEP 1. YOUR SOURCE DISCOVERS A REFERRAL

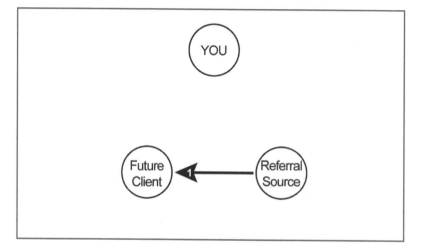

The referral begins with an event that is outside your direct involvement: your referral source uncovers a referral opportunity for you. This occurs without your direct involvement, but it happens because you have laid the groundwork for it by cultivating a mutually beneficial relationship with the person who is going to be motivated to bring you the referral and by making sure she can inform the prospect about the benefits your business can provide.

STEP 2. RESEARCH THE REFERRAL

Your referral source tells you she has a referral for you. At this stage, your impulse might be to call the prospect immediately—you know,

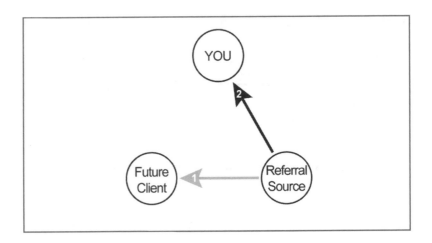

strike while the iron is hot! But that would be a mistake. In fact, it's the most common mistake people make, and in many cases it's referral suicide.

Don't let your excitement cloud your judgment about the opportunity. As soon as you get the call from your referral source, and before you even think of picking up the phone and calling the prospect, you should start digging to find out everything you can about your prospect and his company. How old is the company? What is the prospect's main line of business? How successfully does it compete? What is the company's market valuation? What products or services of yours might be of most use or interest to the company? What is its track record with vendors? Does it deal fairly and straightforwardly with suppliers and clients? Is it in good financial condition? Will you be competing with other vendors for its business?

STEP 3. CHECK BACK IN WITH YOUR REFERRAL SOURCE

After learning all you can about the prospect's company through your outside research, it's a good idea, especially if the referral

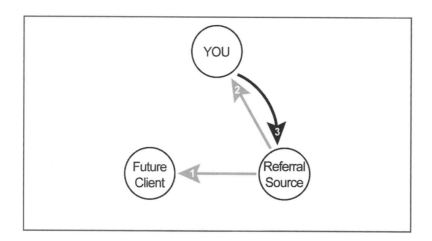

appears to be complex or of very high value, to call your referral source back to confirm or refine what you've learned about the prospect's company.

You need to keep your referral source in the loop and out of trouble. Making her look good is a primary objective, perhaps even more important than the immediate sale, because you want this referral relationship to continue and to benefit both of you far into the future.

More important for your approach to the prospect, you need to know more about him personally, which is something you can assume your referral source is particularly well positioned to help you with.

Try to learn about what sort of individual you'll be dealing with. What's his personality type? Is he detail oriented? If so, he might want to see a lot of collateral material or samples. Is he hard driving and results oriented? He might just want to talk about your offerings, see your track record, and make a quick judgment. Does he like to have fun while doing business? Perhaps you'll join him on the golf course. If he's all business, the office environment is probably better.

What are the prospect's goals? Why is he interested in your products or services? Is he happy with his current provider or

looking for a change? Is he ready to do business with you immediately based on the referral, or is he sending out requests for proposals to other companies?

What you don't want to do is charge at the prospect with no
idea of what is expected or desired. Having some certainty about
these factors will help you put together a powerful presentation
that is tailored to the individual and his company. This will help
you accomplish your two most important objectives: closing the
sale quickly and making your referral source look good.

STEP 4. MEET WITH THE REFERRAL

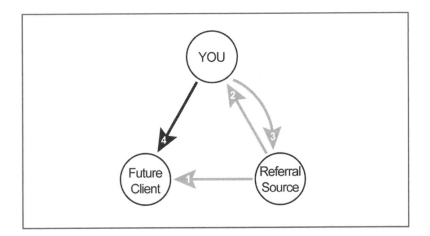

Now comes the move you've been waiting for: your first meeting.
You might close the deal on your first call, but it's unlikely.
Instead, you're probably going to be getting acquainted with your
potential new customer and gathering information to help you
prepare a proposal. Now, what if you could get your referral
source to go along? That would make it a real powerhouse meeting. It would add to your credibility and instantly deepen your
relationship with the prospect.

If you do close the deal at your first meeting, you might think the referral process is over, but in fact it's just started. Before you start turning cartwheels on your way out of the building, call your referral source, tell her what a great referral it was, and thank her for it. Then, when you're back in your office, set your "thank you for the referral" program in motion (see Chapter 26, "Creative Rewards").

STEP 5. REPORT BACK TO YOUR SOURCE

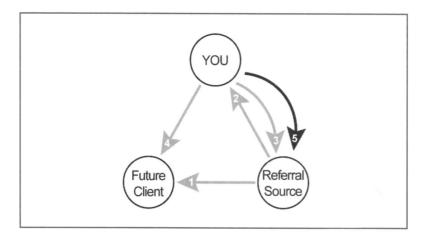

Report back to your referral source and let her know the outcome of your meeting (unless, of course, she went along with you). Ask her to follow up with the prospect to find out about his impression of you. Let her know how important it is for you to make her look good to the prospect.

STEP 6. YOUR SOURCE GETS FEEDBACK FROM THE REFERRAL

The referral source calls your prospect on your behalf to get information that you can use to address any concerns for your next

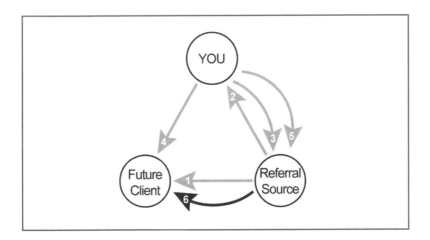

meeting. Since the prospect is likely to tell your source of any concerns that he may not have expressed to you, this is the best way to find out what your prospect is thinking.

STEP 7. YOUR SOURCE REPORTS BACK TO YOU

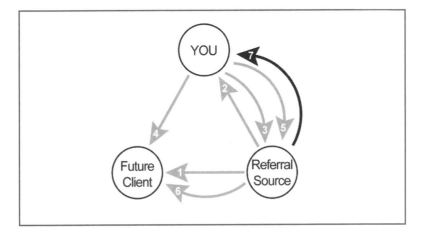

Your source reports back to you with more information about the prospect. This increases your chances of closing the sale on the next call or, if the prospect is already under contract or not currently in the market, perhaps at the next available opportunity. With this information, you can contact the prospect at a more appropriate time and be first in line with a proposal and sales plan ready to go.

STEP 8. CLOSE THE DEAL

Now that you have your proposal done and know all the details, go back to the prospect and close that deal! Once that's done, don't forget to implement your referral thank-you program to inspire your source to continue referring business to you.

You've probably been told that you have to contact most prospects 20 times or more before they will buy. That may be true in ordinary marketing strategies, but in the referral process we've just outlined, the sale often happens in as few as two calls. Didn't close on step 8? No sweat. Just repeat steps 5 through 7 until it's a done deal.

The procedure we've outlined here is a formal, comprehensive referral process, including all the steps you might need to take to fully and properly develop a first-time referral. Many referrals, especially those you make with established contacts, are much simpler; for example, some don't involve a referral source and so require only a couple of steps.

PART V

SECRETS OF
THE MASTERS

CHAPTER

22

Becoming the Knowledgeable Expert

Most businesspeople are at their best in face-to-face meetings with prospects, when they've got notes and sales materials with them and are prepared for the individual they know they'll be meeting. But how can you differentiate yourself during a networking event, when time is short and the next person you meet will be a stranger?

Easy. Think of yourself as the knowledgeable expert—the kind of person who knows a good bit about a particular subject but isn't stingy with that information. A conversation with you about your business should be like talking to your neighbor about his lawn.

"Boy, your lawn looks great," you might say to your neighbor. "What are you using on it?"

"Well, I picked up a bag of Scott's last month and it's really doing the trick. I used to go with the cheaper brand, but it just didn't seem to be working. Anyway, I've been using Scott's for a few weeks now and it's got this lawn looking as good as new. And the best part is it also gets rid of fire ants."

"Really?" you ask.

"Yeah. It was $5.99 a bag down the street. Real easy to put on, too."

"Huh." (Pause.) "So how do you keep all of those weeds back anyway?"

"Well I ran across a product I'm really impressed with," says your neighbor, and he's off describing something else.

Notice how he provided valuable information without overwhelming you. Suppose that in the middle of the conversation, he had casually let drop that he was in the lawn-care business. You'd probably consider his company the next time your yard needed work. Why? Because he obviously knew his stuff, and who wouldn't want to work with an expert in his field? Now imagine yourself doing the same thing when talking to people about challenges in their business that relate to *your* field.

We call such people *knowledgeable experts*, and they're absolute pros in their field. They're the people who know a thing or two about their industry and are happy to share it. They also provide their expertise *without* saying (or even implying), "What's preventing you from making a decision today?" Nobody likes thinly veiled sales questions, and very few prospects ever respond favorably to them.

People are always looking for specific help for specific problems. As a knowledgeable expert with years of experience in your field, you know the challenges your target audience is facing and how best to handle them. You're intimately familiar with what works and what doesn't. Most of all, you know what it takes to get stuff done.

But how do you demonstrate this to prospects while networking, *before* you've asked for a sit-down meeting or even followed up over the phone? Easy: *by staying on top of the industry news.* In previous books we've often talked about the virtues of reading and constantly educating yourself about your industry; here's where that time really pays off.

A good way to become the knowledgeable expert in the eyes of your potential prospects is to have a feel for some of the other networking events around town and how those events might relate to *their* business. Let's say that during a conversation at a chamber event one evening a photographer tells you she's trying to meet people in advertising and public relations. You might mention that the local business owners' association holds networking events once a month and that, even though you haven't been there personally, you understand this is where ad people and marketing directors go to network. This is valuable information for your prospect—and it's valuable for you, too, because it makes you a knowledgeable resource and makes you stand out from the crowd.

Another way to parlay good information into your day-to-day networking is to become versed on a few statistics that are relevant to your prospects. For example, if you're a financial planner and you're talking with someone who expresses concern about her retirement plan, it might be good to know that three out of five working professionals *won't* have enough money to retire on by the age of 65, according to Randy Brunson, Certified Financial Planner (CFP), Centurion Advisor Group. Then you can follow up with a personal anecdote on how you helped a client overcome similar challenges toward securing his own financial peace of mind (notice the choice of words). Now you're well on your way to becoming the knowledgeable expert in your prospect's eyes. Why? Because you're giving her good information on how she can personally overcome a situation that's affecting millions of people each day.

Another way to become a knowledgeable expert is to be familiar with your prospect's issues. What are her concerns? What are her specific challenges? As a financial planner, you might learn that your prospect doesn't understand the stock market and generally distrusts the financial information that companies publish. Like the rest of us, she's seen how millions of stockholders have been defrauded by corporate malfeasance and stock manipulation. She might have real concerns about investing. This is where you can help by providing reliable information to allay her concerns:

> *That's an excellent point, Mrs. Smith, and believe it or not, according to a recent survey by the Centurion Advisory Group, financially fraudulent information was only involved in less than 1 percent of the total transactions conducted last year. Couple that with our firm's strict policy of full disclosure on all financial transactions, and you can see how we've worked hard to gain the trust of all our clients.*

Stating facts this way can give your prospect the peace of mind she's looking for, since it shows an understanding for her concern along with a willingness to allay that fear with good, sound data. One simple statistic can help ratchet up your credibility with a relatively new contact, and it all starts by having an understanding of what your prospect's true concerns are.

Or suppose that you're a mortgage broker, and someone at a chamber says, "So what is it you do?"

"I specialize in helping people get into the home of their dreams, regardless of past credit history," you say.

"Really," he responds. "Regardless of history, huh? I always thought credit was everything when it came to financing a home."

"Well, sure, great credit is going to make my job a whole lot easier. But there are lots of ways to finance a home, without necessarily having the best credit in the world. Something I advise my clients to close out any unnecessary credit cards. Even if they have a zero balance, they can hurt your credit score when it comes to getting a loan. That, plus a solid payment history on the cards you do have, is usually enough to get you in the door—literally and figuratively."

"Is that so?"

"Oh, yes. As a matter of fact, I was working a file the other day where a couple were coming out of a bankruptcy, and because of that they were having a tough time finding financing. A mutual friend of ours knew about the situation, referred me in, and within a couple of weeks we were working on a program I think will do the trick."

"Really?" (Pause.) "Let me get your card. I've got someone you might want to meet."

And there you go.

Notice how you were able to clearly demonstrate your expertise in a subtle, yet powerful manner? The conversation didn't feel like a pitch, just a comfortable exchange of good information in which you clearly showed that you know what you're doing. This, needless to say, will make that prospect feel more inclined to work with you.

One of the questions we often get in workshops is this: "Is it possible that I will give away too much good information and wind up not converting this new contact into a client?" Great question, since that obviously defeats the purpose of networking in the first place. Here's what we recommend: when networking, focus on demonstrating your ability to handle the problem, without giving your prospect everything he needs to know to solve it.

It's not that hard to become a knowledgeable expert. Just take a minute to read an article about your industry once a day,

BRIAN

I usually talk about the prospect's business and some different things he could do to bring in more revenue. Since I'm a marketing coach by trade, my conversations always seem to gravitate toward helping others get more business. So after hearing some of their issues, throwing out some general ideas, and sharing a couple of personal stories demonstrating my expertise, I might wrap up with something like this:

> Well, if we decided to work together, one of the things I'd recommend is to take a look at your business and identify two or three specific audiences, or target markets, that are most likely to use your services. You mentioned how you feel exhausted at the end of the day, working hard and doing a bunch of good things. But sometimes it's hard to pinpoint exactly what you're accomplishing.
>
> Having some specific target markets will help you get away from that, so you don't have to feel like you're always running around from one networking event to the other, chasing the latest lead. You can have a crystal-clear focus on the people you want to meet and where they're most likely to be, which by itself should be a real boost for your business.
>
> After that, I'd want to see some of your brochures and other marketing collateral. I know you mentioned that you just updated your website, and that's a great first step toward getting more

business. I'm thinking maybe an electronic newsletter that gets people visiting your site would be a good idea, along with a link that gives them an opportunity to look at your brochure.

Obviously we don't have time to get into that right now, but if you'd like, I can take your card, give you a call in a few days, and if we want to set up some time to talk more about this, that's absolutely fine.

In this way, I am able to incorporate our conversation into a workable game plan on what I'd recommend if we decided to work together. And when the game plan is mentioned at the end of the conversation, after you've stated relevant statistics and after you've demonstrated understanding of the prospect's issues, it's almost impossible not to be seen as the knowledgeable expert—and get a lot more business in the process.

perhaps online where you can easily keep up with current developments. Familiarize yourself with it; remember a specific fact or statistic that you can work into a networking conversation. Then you're good to go.

With buyers' skepticism at an all-time high, people are going to give you business only *after* you've made them comfortable with your expertise. The way to do that is to fill yourself up with as much knowledge as possible about your prospects' challenges, along with stories demonstrating how you've helped others in the past. When you're the knowledgeable expert, you're the go-to guy (or gal)!

23

Networking at Non-Networking Events

Most of what we've discussed so far is about networking in traditional networking venues, such as the chamber, strong-contact referral groups, and other business-oriented gatherings. But if you think that's all networking is about, then you're not using its power to its fullest.

You can network anywhere, including events where it might not at first occur to you to try it—and, paradoxically, it's at these nontraditional networking settings where you'll get the most bang for your buck. Why? Because not many people think of it.

You've got the field to yourself, with many opportunities to develop lasting relationships with potential referral partners.

PERSON TO PERSON

What nontraditional settings are we referring to? Well, everybody goes to parties, and the holiday season is full of them. It's also a business slowdown season for many of us who are not in retail. Although networking is not just a New Year's Day-to-Thanksgiving activity—it's year-round—holiday parties and other social mixers bring new opportunities to network, even more than the rest of the year.

When we tell people this, we usually get strange looks. They think of boorish sharpies selling time-shares to your aunt and uncle at your grandparents' 50th wedding anniversary or trying to round up business at funerals. But networking is not just trying to sell something or passing business referrals; it's building meaningful relationships and social capital. Master networkers understand this. That's why they're always networking.

You're already in a relationship with everybody you know. The only question is how developed that relationship is (see Chapter 17, "How Deep Is Your Network?"). Is it a relationship of visibility, in which you know each other but haven't had dealings? Is it one of credibility, in which you've interacted enough to have established a degree of mutual trust? Or has it deepened over time to the point of profitability, with both parties receiving mutual benefits as a result of assistance, business referrals, or other interactions?

In today's environment, it's easy for us to lose that personal touch when we do so much of our communicating via email and cell phone. The fact is, most relationships develop through physical presence in one-to-one interactions and get stronger every time we meet face-to-face. The holidays are times when we are more likely to see people in a social setting, and this setting definitely lends itself to building relationships. There are, however, some things that are important when networking at a holiday social—or at any event, for that matter.

ASK, "HOW CAN I HELP?"

Givers Gain is the number-one rule to remember. You should always be thinking, "How can I help this person?" Many of us know this and try to apply it to our relationships, but we're more inclined to do it instinctively with those in the profitability category. How can we apply it to the relationships that are in the visibility and credibility categories?

At a social event, you usually ask somebody, "How's it going?" What's the typical reply? Probably something like "Great; things couldn't be better." That's a canned response that people give because they want to be polite and because they know nobody really wants to hear their troubles. But it's not usually the whole truth.

IVAN

Things can always be better—that is, there are surely ways you can help—but most people aren't inclined to go into detail or let others know what's going on, especially at social events. The best way to find out is to avoid generalities like "How are things?" Ask more specific questions.

In a conversation I had recently, I asked an individual how things were going and got the standard answer that things were great, the company was expanding, and business was better than expected. My next question was "Are you hitting all of your goals?" Yes, the business was exceeding all of its goals by a large margin.

Sounds like this person didn't need any help, you say? On the contrary: to me it sounded like a big opportunity. Think about it: a company that was expanding faster than the owner had projected. What kind of help might it need?

Many consider networking just another way to get clients, but when you think in terms of building relationships, a chance to help is a big opportunity. That help can be provided in many forms, each as valuable as the next.

In this case I was able to make some introductions that the individual was very grateful for. But it was only after getting past the generalities that I was able to figure this out.

Always plan on maximizing your networking productivity during the holiday season. Remember, networking means developing relationships, and the holidays are filled with opportunity.

BE SINCERE

If you're networking successfully at a non-networking event, people won't even know it. You're genuinely looking for ways to help other people, and your concern for the person you're talking with is plainly apparent. Anyone who is networking exclusively for personal gain comes across as shallow and insincere.

A good networker doesn't have to work at sincerity. She really cares about making connections for others, not just for herself. Some people are so accomplished and successful at networking that they are able to network virtually anywhere. No one minds your using an opportunity to share information that will benefit others, even when that exchange takes the form of a business card at a bar mitzvah.

HONOR THE EVENT

Always remember to respect the event you're attending. This one should be a no-brainer, but we all know some scorched-earth, overzealous networkers who trawl the room at a party in pursuit of a sale, any sale. They may do the same, less blatantly, at family and purely social events, but this is still the exact opposite of what networking is all about. Remember, relationships are the name of the game. Socials are a great place to get visibility and credibility, so focus on building these aspects of relationships.

24

Becoming a Referral Gatekeeper

After you've been networking for a while, you begin to see that there's a pattern to the all those connections you've been making. It's as if you're sitting in the middle of a spider web, with all the lines running outward connected to other lines, and whenever someone you're connected to makes a connection for you, you can feel the vibrations coming in from that direction. What's really happening, though, is that each person you're connected to is at the center of a web of his own.

Once you visualize how complex this web really is, you may begin to think, "What if I could be more directly connected to all those other webs out there? Would I get more referrals? Would I get a greater variety of referrals? Would I get higher-quality referrals? Is there a species of supernetworker who is in direct contact with those other networkers, the ones who are connected to me only through intermediaries?"

GUARDIAN AT THE GATE

The answer is yes, there is a special type of networker who is more connected than most: the referral gatekeeper.

IVAN

When I started my first business, I knew I wanted referrals to play a key part in my overall growth strategy. The only problem was I didn't know exactly what I needed to do to accomplish that goal. So I joined some business associations, started networking more, and did everything I could to generate more word-of-mouth marketing. Though all of that worked to a large extent, it finally dawned on me how I could supercharge the whole process.

I began to realize that I wasn't the only one trying to get more sales through referrals; a lot of other business professionals were trying to do the same thing. But it also occurred to me that the people I knew were different from the people the next person knew, who were different from the next person's contacts, and so on. I might get a few referrals from my own network, but I could probably get a few more referrals from the other person's network, and the ones beyond that, almost without limit.

So I thought, "What if I became the hub?" If all the other people out there were trying to do the same thing as I was, why couldn't I position myself as a gatekeeper of sorts between other people's networks? Then, if someone was buying a new home and needed a real estate agent but didn't have one in her own network, she would come to me to see whom I knew.

How did that help my business?

First, it encouraged me to continue building and deepening my relationships with others, even if I didn't think they could help me right away. Let's face it: we are all limited on time, and our natural tendency is to build relationships with those we feel can help us the most. No problem, except for one thing: you never know whom the other person knows.

Even though it might not appear that way on the surface, it's always a good idea to have a lot of contacts. Becoming a gatekeeper gave me another good reason to do just that. Bob Smith might not be a good referral partner for me, but he could be ideal for Jane Doe, another person I know.

The second reason I thought this would be good for my business was the positive effect it would have on my credibility. I wanted to be the go-to guy in the business community—the person others came to if they needed a referral for anything. This meant that I would be deepening relationships with people I might not otherwise have gotten to know. Furthermore, since we all know people do business with others they like and trust, who do you think is going to get their business when they need someone like me? You got it.

With all this in mind, I drafted the following letter:

Dear _____:

I really believe in the process of referrals, and so part of the service I provide is to be sure to refer my clients and associates to other qualified businesspeople in the community.

Attached is a list of areas in which I know very credible, ethical, and outstanding professionals. If you're looking for a professional in a specific area I've listed, please feel free to contact me. I will be glad to put you in touch with the people I know who provide these services.

Sincerely,

Dr. Ivan Misner

Notice, when reading this letter, that I listed only professions; I didn't list names and phone numbers. I wanted my clients to contact me so I could put the referral and the contact together. I wanted to build relationships, not to become a glorified phone directory. I wanted to become known as an effective networker, and that would happen only if I made the connections myself.

Essentially, I wanted to deepen the relationships I had with my clients so they would be more likely to keep me as their service provider of choice. In our BNI groups, we say that every relationship is in one of three phases—visibility, credibility, or profitability. Obviously you want to move as many people as quickly as possible into the profitability phase. And that's what this letter enabled me to do. I mailed it to all my clients (and prospects) four times in the first year. I didn't get a single reply until the third time, but after that, the floodgates opened and I got responses every time I sent it out.

Over time, I cultivated a reputation as a gatekeeper by doing this. I no longer had to send out my letter several times a year. People came to see me because they heard I knew a great number of businesspeople in the community. Others would ask people on my client list, "Whom do you know who does XYZ?" If my contacts didn't know anyone, they would send the questioner to me.

If you are a businessperson seeking to grow your business by word-of-mouth marketing, becoming a gatekeeper will give you an enormous advantage. It's a strategy that not only gets people to contact you for referrals but also opens up a dialogue with them about your business and how it can help them. This, in turn, leads to more business with existing clients and new business with prospects.

On the other side of the process, the people on my list of professions, the ones to whom I referred potential customers, were impressed and grateful. They reciprocated by sending people my way, and they began to come to me when they needed a referral. It helped, of course, that I had sent each of them a copy of my letter to tell them I would be sending business their way.

As I developed my mailing list, I would drop certain people off it with whom I didn't have any further contact. One time someone who had been dropped from my list called to tell me he missed the letters! He needed a referral and had to look up an old letter of mine he had kept on file. I actually ended up doing some business with him as a result of this incident.

This is just one technique to consider when building your business through referrals. It's a touch point that puts you in contact with your clients and prospects in a way that fosters different dynamics than when you're trying to sell to them. You have something they need: referrals and contacts. Allow this to open the door for reciprocal sharing and giving. You'll be amazed at how much more business you can do with each other as a result.

HUB OF THE WHEEL

Another way to be a referral gatekeeper is to position your business as a hub firm. This is a familiar concept to experienced business networkers and is a good way to take advantage of the nature of your business if your line of work involves routine contact with other businesses. If you're a financial planner, for instance, your work with a client might involve putting him in contact with an investment counselor, a stockbroker, an insurance agent, a tax planner, and so forth. A building contractor is another familiar example; among the firms that orbit this hub are plumbers, electricians, air conditioner installers, cement companies, roofers, and many others.

Here's another example: Suppose you're a wedding planner. Your business puts you in constant contact with a number of other businesses that relate to weddings: caterers, bakers, florists, photographers, jewelers, wedding chapels, and others. You can envision your business as the hub of a wheel (see Figure 24.1).

Depending on the size and cost of the wedding, you may be in touch with different combinations of these other businesses. An expensive wedding might have you signing contracts with businesses A, C, D, E, G, and H; a less elaborate ceremony might involve only companies B, D, and F. Even though you work with

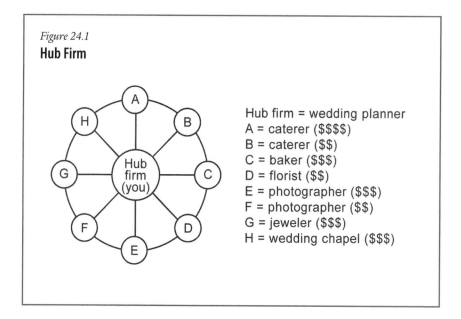

Figure 24.1
Hub Firm

Hub firm = wedding planner
A = caterer ($$$$)
B = caterer ($$)
C = baker ($$$)
D = florist ($$)
E = photographer ($$$)
F = photographer ($$)
G = jeweler ($$$)
H = wedding chapel ($$$)

business that compete with each other, you become a referral partner with every one of them because you refer businesses to all of them over time.

Being a hub firm makes you a very powerful networker. In fact, putting yourself at the center of any network can make you a master networker in short order, able to choose the cream of the high-quality clients that will come your way.

25

Being Your Own Chief Networking Officer

I f you work in an organization you might be familiar with the increasingly popular position of chief networking officer (CNO). The CNO is the person who handles many corporations' business networking and community-related activities.

The role or position of CNO has changed over the years. In the past the CNO could have been the person responsible for such things as running the computer or IT department, or for computer-related functions in general, because networking was thought of as a matter of electronic connection. CNOs are still tech related, but these days we're seeing many executives with that title in charge of completely different functions, handling business networking activities such as these:

- Community involvement
- Internal communication
- External communication
- Public relations
- Corporate culture
- Social capital
- Human resources

- Diversity
- Client/customer relationships
- Developing a word-of-mouth campaign
- Departmental collaboration
- Relationship advertising and marketing
- Improving vendor relationships
- Referral generation strategies

As you can see, a CNO's responsibilities can be broad and complex. We focus on just two here: 1) word-of-mouth campaigns and 2) referral generation strategies. These roles should be top of mind if you're going to network like a pro. They should be the principal job focus of your CNO.

First, however, let's address the thought that's probably just popped into your head: "Hey, it's just a ten-person (four-person/one-person) organization; how can I afford to hire a CNO to do my networking?"

As business professionals ourselves, we remember what it was like trying to get a company off the ground. And quite frankly, there never seemed to be enough resources to take care of all the things the business needed, let alone hire an executive-level person.

What we're suggesting is creating a CNO position in your company and then filling it yourself, at least in the beginning. In other words, don't hire a CNO; just take on a CNO mind-set.

How do you create a CNO mind-set? Start off by adopting a Givers Gain attitude. This gets you in the spirit of finding ways to help others while simultaneously overcoming the scarcity mentality that can creep into your thinking. Lay out a clear set of guidelines and action items that you'd like the CNO to take, and then fill that position yourself for two or three hours a week.

IVAN

In his book *The eMyth*, Michael Gerber talks about the importance of creating clearly defined job descriptions within a company—bookkeeper, marketing person, chief cook, and bottle washer—so all employees understand their roles and responsibilities.

He goes on to say that even if your name is under all of those positions (which is often the case for most small businesses), the goal is to reach a point where you can bring in other people to do some of those jobs for you. By having a clear job description already in place, your transition from *being in the business to managing the business* becomes a whole lot smoother. If you haven't yet read this book, I'd highly recommend it.

Here are some actions you can take day to day.

ATTEND A FEW NETWORKING EVENTS EACH MONTH AND FOLLOW UP

As a smart, enterprising businessperson, you already know the importance of networking and how vital it is to meet new people. (We recommend attending two to three events each month to generate new contacts.) However, one of the biggest mistakes people make is failing to follow up. (Yes, we know you have places to go and things to do.)

By adopting a CNO mind-set, you recognize that meeting new folks while networking is just the first step toward generating more word-of-mouth business. The second step is meeting them later over coffee or lunch to learn more about their business and how you can help them. When you do that, you pave the way for future referral business. (For more on what to say when following up with someone you just met, see Chapter 19.)

REGULARLY TOUCH BASE WITH PAST BUSINESS CONTACTS

We suggest keeping in touch with past business contacts by making two personal phone calls each week. Again, if you're like us, you've got so much going on that the thought of making two more phone calls is almost too much. But remember, a CNO's job

BRIAN

I was making some of these base-touching calls one day when I found myself talking to a good friend of mine whose organization had invited me to speak on several occasions. I knew the group had just concluded a conference the week before, and I wanted to catch up with my friend and see how things went. We chatted for a few minutes, he gave me the scoop on what the attendees wanted from the following year's event, and just like that, I had the inside track on speaking at their next conference.

I achieved this result not because I was specifically trying get that deal (I didn't even know the opportunity existed) but because I wanted to stay in touch with a good business contact. Lo and behold, it turned into a referral right there on the spot.

is maintaining relationships and generating referrals. And that can't happen unless you stay in touch.

USE CARDS TO STAY IN TOUCH THROUGHOUT THE YEAR

A good time to send postcards or greeting cards is on annual holidays—and not just Christmas or New Year's, but also St. Patrick's Day (March), Memorial Day (May), Independence Day (July), Labor Day (September), and Halloween (October), when a card can be an unexpected surprise.

You can start off by buying a pack of 20 cards and sending them to people you've fallen out of touch with or with whom you'd like to reconnect—past clients, past vendors, a friend of a friend, another business owner you chatted with at your local coffee shop a few months ago. Doing this will keep you top of mind with these people in a unique way. Your note could read something like this:

> *John—*
>
> *We met a few months ago at the chamber of commerce. Things have been really busy here lately, but I wanted to take a minute and wish you and your family a safe and happy July Fourth.*
>
> *As a matter of fact, how about I give you a call in a week or two and see what our calendars look like? I'd be interested in learning more about your business and, who knows, I might even be able to refer you some clients. I look forward to catching up.*
>
> *Joe Smith*

TAKE GOOD CARE OF YOUR DATABASE

With all this talk about phone calls and greeting cards, it makes sense that a CNO should have a top-flight contact database and contact management system (CMS) to help her stay organized and on top of things. A contact database is simply a storage facility enabling you to keep track of all the people you've met. It can be as simple as a physical card file or as high-tech as an online data site. It just needs to be something you can use so business cards aren't falling off your desk and onto the floor.

Using database management software can streamline and supercharge your referral generation system. Because there are data entry fields for many different kinds of information (e-mail address, phone number, profession, where you met the contact, etc.), you can sort contacts by many different criteria and target emails to particular segments of your database with a few clicks of the mouse. We have experience with several such systems, including ACT, Microsoft Outlook, and Relate2Profit.com.

The reason these systems are so important for a CNO is because his contacts are his business! You can't get referrals unless you have relationships, and you can't have relationships unless you stay in touch and up-to-date with contacts. Having a good contact database and contact management system enables you to do both while creating a powerful word-of-mouth marketing campaign.

ALWAYS THANK YOUR REFERRAL PARTNERS

A referral partner is not simply a contact who gives you referrals every once in a while; a referral partner is someone with whom you have entered into a relationship that is mutually trusting, respectful, and beneficial. Maintaining that relationship means, among other things, thanking your contact for referrals. It's not only good manners but also good for keeping the benefits mutual.

Thanks can and often should take the form of reciprocation, of course; get a referral, give a referral. The law of reciprocity, however, doesn't require such a quid pro quo response, and indeed it might even seem a bit artificial if it happened as a matter of course. The person being thanked might be inclined to think, "If my partner can send me one referral every time I send him a referral, how many might he be able to send me if he sent me all the business he knows I could use? Is he, in other words, holding back? Is he doling them out like dog treats every time I perform a trick?"

Rather than foster such ideas, make sure you send your partner a referral every time you have the opportunity; chances are the ones you receive from him (and others) will balance out in the long run. Gratitude by reciprocity should be given freely and abundantly and not in measured response to the number of referrals received. A referral partnership should never be viewed as a simple accountancy.

A simple "thank you" is always appreciated and should always be the first response given. It's probably the single biggest action a CNO can take to maximize the number of referrals he gets. It will typically double the amount of referral business he gets from an existing referral partner.

This simple thanks can take many forms other than a voiced "thank you." For other ideas on how you can express your thanks, read Chapter 26, "Creative Rewards" and Appendix I, "Credibility-Enhancing Materials." For the present, simply understand that thanking the person who gave you a referral in the first place is just as important as getting that referral. When you do, that person will be more likely to do it again and provide another revenue boost for your business.

Creative
Rewards

Most people would agree that one of the best ways to consistently generate referrals is to have a system that rewards your referral partners. There are many ways you can do this, but the best way is to design creative incentives for them. However, of all the techniques for making the system work, this one seems to frustrate people the most.

The most common incentive for referrals is a finder's fee. Although a finder's fee can work in some situations, it might not be best approach with every referral partner. Why? Because when a trusted referral partner gives you a referral, it's usually the by-product of your good relationship, and an offer of money would tend to cheapen the experience; it might even be considered an insult.

However, this doesn't mean generosity should go unrewarded. You just need to find a more creative way to say thanks.

IVAN

Years ago I went to my chiropractor for a routine adjustment. I had referred a friend to him several weeks before who had recently been in an accident. As I walked into the waiting room, I noticed a bulletin board displayed prominently on the wall. The bulletin board read, "We would like to thank the following patients for referring someone to us last month."

There was nothing unusual about this sign; it had been there on each of my previous visits. But this time my name was on it. I took notice and was pleased but didn't give it a second thought—until a month later, when I returned and saw that my name was no longer on it. Instantly I thought, "Who else can I refer to the doctor so my name will be put back on the board?" For the record, I did come up with another referral for the good doctor.

Being highlighted on a bulletin board might not work for everyone, but if it worked on me, I'm sure it has a positive effect on others as well, for at least two reasons. The bulletin board is a continual reminder to patients that the office wants their referrals, and people like to be recognized for their efforts.

There are many ways to reward people for referrals, depending on the type of product or service you offer and your relationship with your referring parties. The key is to offer rewards that are attractive to as many people as possible. Some health-care professionals offer a free visit when a referral becomes a new patient. Business professionals sometimes send small gift baskets, bottles of wine, flowers, or certificates for their services or the services of other businesses in the community. Other professionals offer free estimates, samples, or analyses, discounts on products or services, group discounts, or even extended warranties.

One enterprising business professional offered clients who brought him good referrals a $500 discount on their next purchase. This was a bargain. A new customer is worth many times that amount in business, and the cost of advertising, printed literature, and time spent on telephone calls, meetings, appointments, and sales calls that are typically needed to bring in a new customer can far exceed the cost of such a referral incentive. You can afford to be generous with a good referral partner, who can readily bring you more business. Incentive programs also help you sell more products or services to your existing customer base with little effort or marketing cost.

Some businesspeople use a technique known as *incentive triangulation*, a powerful way of leveraging other people's services to benefit your customers, clients, or patients. The concept is simple and can be designed to fit the needs or requirements of almost any business.

Here's how it works. First, you negotiate an arrangement with another local business—printer, massage therapist, jeweler,

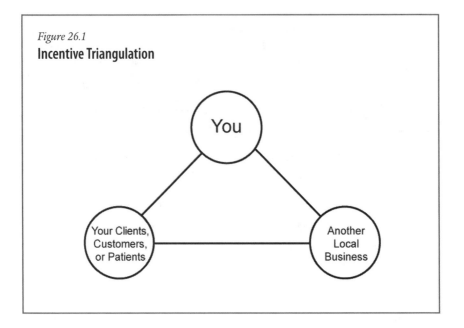

Figure 26.1
Incentive Triangulation

florist—to give a discount to any of your clients you send its way. Then, whenever one of your clients gives you a referral, you reward that person with your usual incentive, plus a coupon good for your prearranged discount at the other business. (See Figure 26.1.)

This form of joint venture is beneficial for all three parties. You benefit because you are providing another incentive for people to give you referrals. The other business benefits because you are recommending it to your clients. Your referrer benefits because she gets recognition for her efforts, as well as an additional product or service at a reduced rate. Granted, this type of incentive may not be appropriate for all professions, but when it works, it works well.

No matter what form of incentive program you use, the fact that you offer incentives increases your potential for generating word-of-mouth business. The question is, what type of incentive will work for you? To meet the challenge of finding the right incentive program, tap into the assistance and insights of other people. An effective way to do this is to invite about ten people you know to meet with you over lunch or dinner. Include a representative sample of your customers (or clients or patients), business associates, partners, and friends. Tell them their assignment is to think up incentives you could offer to increase your word-of-mouth-based business.

Prepare yourself well in advance. Be prepared to take copious notes or to tape-record the meeting. Think about the topic and its ramifications; have an idea of the limits you may need to set for an incentive program, such as cost, duration, and appropriateness. Have soft drinks, note pads, a preliminary questionnaire, sample materials, a flip chart, and even a few ideas to get the ball rolling. If you're going to discuss a product, bring samples to give the group a point of reference.

Begin the session by clearly stating a specific problem. Make sure your group understands that the incentive has to be geared to the group you've targeted. Explain that you are looking for a variety of ideas and that you won't make any immediate decisions.

When your group meets, the first step is to brainstorm ideas. The concept of brainstorming was originated by Alex F. Osborn to help trigger creative ideas in advertising. Following the meal, you or a designated party can lead a brainstorming session to generate ideas on an effective incentive program for your business. For maximum creativity, everyone must fully understand and follow four basic principles. To paraphrase Osborn:

1. *Encourage freewheeling.* The wilder the ideas, the better; it's easier to tame down ideas than to think them up. Wild ideas often lead to creative solutions, but the way an idea is first presented by its originator doesn't always register with others. With a twist and turn, however, ideas seemingly from Mars are brought back to Earth and become eminently workable.
2. *The more, the better.* The greater the number of ideas people think of, the better the likelihood of a winner coming out

of the selection. Don't be afraid to go to the second or third page of a flip chart. You want at least 12 ideas so you'll have plenty to work with once everyone runs out of steam.

3. *Don't rush to judgment.* Criticism of ideas must be withheld until later; otherwise you run the risk of shutting down the idea pipeline. Not only does criticism stifle creativity, but it can make the session deteriorate to a nitpicking session that goes on forever without accomplishing anything.

4. *Combine and refine.* In addition to contributing ideas of their own, participants should suggest how ideas of others could be turned into better ideas, or how two or more ideas could be combined into still another idea. Some ideas that aren't workable alone become quite effective in combination.

Once you've run out of new ideas for possible incentives, review the list item by item and try to narrow it down to a manageable number. Don't worry about how you're going to do something until you've determined all the options. After most of the ideas are eliminated, spend time discussing those that are left and get feedback on which ones may be most effective. Last, select the idea or ideas you'll put into practice.

At the end of the session, if the ideas were really flying, suggest the group meet again soon. Instead of having a one- or two-time session, your group might even become an advisory board, meeting at regular intervals. Even if you meet only quarterly or semiannually, there is great value in having reconvened to discuss the challenges you're working on.

Creativity is the key to any good incentive program. People just naturally like to help each other, especially when they know their efforts are successful. Let your contact know when a referral he has made comes through, and be as creative as you can. There are many creative ways businesspeople reward those who send them referrals. A female consultant sends bouquets of flowers to men; a music store owner sends concert tickets; a financial planner sends change purses and money clips.

An accountant in St. Louis thanks those who successfully refer a client to him by paying for a dinner for two at an exclusive restaurant that's at least an hour's drive from their homes. This approach firmly plants the accountant in the minds of his referral sources: They won't be able to use the reward right away, because the distance requires that they plan for it. As the date approaches, because it has been planned, they'll be talking about it and probably about the accountant. Later, when the referring party runs into someone else who might need an accountant, whom do you think he'll recommend?

IVAN

Almost 20 years ago, a real estate agent I met in northern California told me that for almost six years he had offered a $100 finder's fee to anyone giving him a referral that led to a listing or sale. He said that in all that time he had given only about a dozen finder's fees, so he decided to try another kind of incentive.

Living on a large parcel of land in prime wine country, he had begun growing grapes in his own vineyard. A thought occurred to him: Why not take the next step? He began processing the grapes and bottling his own special vintage wine. After his first harvest, he had a graphic artist design a beautiful label, which he affixed to each bottle. He told all his friends that he did not sell this wine; he gave it as a gift to anyone providing him with a bona fide referral.

He gave away dozens of cases in the first three years—half the time it took him to give only one dozen cash finder's fees—yet each bottle cost him less than $10 to produce. This special vintage wine makes him infinitely more money than giving away a handful of $100 finder's fees.

About two weeks ago, I got a call from the real estate agent, who told me the following story. A woman he didn't know called him and gave him two referrals. As he wrote down the information, he asked her how she had heard of him. She said she had had dinner one night at a friend's house. She had complimented the host on his wine selection and asked him where he'd gotten it. He told her it was not found in any store, that the only way to get a bottle was to give a referral to a real estate agent he knew. She got his contact information from her friend and called him up two days later.

After giving the real estate agent the referrals, she said, "I have two referrals. Can I get two bottles?" He told me he sent her the bottles, and both referrals turned into business, each costing him only $10.

Now, if you're wondering how something as simple as a bottle of wine can be such a powerful incentive for giving referrals, the explanation is really quite simple: it's special. A bottle of wine that can't be bought can be worth ten times what it costs to produce when traded for something as valuable as a business referral.

Another option to keep in mind is to offer different kinds of incentives for different groups of people. Are there employees, co-workers, friends, or relatives who might be able to refer you business? It always surprises us when people forget to provide incentives for the individuals working with them. You may choose to offer something completely different for your employees than you would for your clients or networking associates. Bonuses and vacation days are always a good idea, but the important thing is you need to offer something for them as well.

Remember, finding the right incentive is considered the biggest challenge by most individuals who want to build their word-of-mouth business. To make it easier on yourself, be sure to get opinions and feedback from others who have a significant interest in your success.

Take a few minutes to review the Networking Like a Pro Game Plan (Appendix II). This will help you prepare your own personal incentive program. Don't underestimate the value of recognizing and thanking your referral partners; they're the people who send you business.

PART VI

IS YOUR NETWORKING WORKING?

27

Top Ten Ways Others Can Promote You

Has anyone ever said to you, "If there's anything I can do to help you with your business, let me know"?

And was your response "Thank you. Now that you mention it, there are a few things I need"? Or did you say, "Well, thanks, I'll let you know"?

If you're like most of us, you aren't prepared to accept help at the moment it's offered. Before you can do so, you have to make the connection between specific items or services you need and the people who can supply them.

Systematic referral marketing helps you do that by determining, as precisely as possible, the types of help you want and need. Some are simple, cheap, and quick; others are complex, costly, and time-consuming. Here are some examples of the ways others can promote you and your business.

1. *Display or distribute your literature and products.* Your sources can exhibit your marketing materials and products in their offices or homes. If these items are displayed well, such as on a counter or a bulletin board, visitors will ask questions about them or read the information. Some may take your promotional materials and display them in other places, increasing your visibility. They can include your fliers in their mailings or hand them out at meetings they attend. A dry cleaner attaches a coupon from the hair salon next door to each plastic bag he uses to cover his customers' clothing; a grocery store includes other businesses' marketing literature in or on its grocery bags or on the back of the printed receipt.

2. *Make an announcement.* When attending meetings or speaking to groups, your sources can increase your visibility by announcing an event you are involved in or a sale your business is conducting, or by setting up exhibits of your products or services. They can also invite you to make an announcement yourself.

3. *Invite you to attend events.* Workshops and seminars are opportunities to increase your skills, knowledge, visibility, and contacts. Members of personal or business groups you don't belong to can invite you to their events and programs, which gives you an opportunity to meet prospective sources and clients. Even better, they could invite you to speak at their event, effectively positioning you as an expert in your field.

4. *Endorse your products and services.* By telling others what they've gained from using your products or services or by endorsing you in presentations or informal conversations,

your network sources can encourage others to use your products or services. If they sing your praises on a CD, MP3, or DVD, so much the better.

5. *Nominate you for recognition and awards.* Business professionals and community members often are recognized for outstanding service to their profession or community. If you've donated time or materials to a worthy cause, your referral sources can nominate you for service awards. You increase your visibility both by serving and by receiving the award in a public expression of thanks. Your sources can inform others of your recognition by word of mouth or in writing. They can even create an award, such as Vendor of the Month, to honor your achievement.

6. *Make initial contact with prospects and referral sources.* Instead of just giving you the telephone number and address of an important prospect, a network member can phone or meet the prospect first and tell him about you. When you make contact with the prospect, he will be expecting to hear from you and will know something about you. Better yet, your source can help you build new relationships faster through a personal introduction to that person. Ideally she would provide you with key information about the prospect while also telling the prospect a few things about you, your business, and some of the things you and the prospect have in common.

7. *Arrange a meeting on your behalf.* When one of your sources tells you about a person you should meet or someone you consider a key contact, she can help you immensely by coordinating a meeting. Ideally, she will not only call the contact and set a specific date, time, and location for the meeting but will also attend the meeting with you.

8. *Publish information for you.* Network members may be able to get information about you and your business printed in

publications they subscribe to and in which they have some input or influence. For example, a referral source who belongs to an association that publishes a newsletter might help you get an article published or persuade the editor to run a story about you. Many companies showcase topic-specific experts in their newsletters; you could become the expert in your field for some of these.

9. *Form strategic alliances with you.* Of all the kinds of support that a source can offer, this one has the greatest potential for long-term gain for both parties. When you engage in a strategic alliance, you're in essence developing a formal relationship with another business owner that says you will refer him business whenever possible and he will do the same. This works best in businesses that are complementary. For example, a handyman would find advantages in forming an alliance with a real estate agents, because they continually encounter people who need home repair work done. Conversely, a handyman probably deals with homeowners who are considering selling their homes after he's finished making repairs. Such strategic alliances can work with a number of other businesses (CPAs and financial advisors, mortgage brokers and real estate agents, hotel salespeople and event planners, and so on). The key is to find the person with the right complementary business and then make it work for both of you.

10. *Connect with you through online networks.* When people connect with you online, you can notify them about your events or projects, and you can receive the same kind of information from them. They can see your business profile and biographic data and can refer you to people in their networks. Once connected, they can provide recommendations and testimonials for the rest of your network to view.

28

Ten Levels of Referrals

A referral is a referral, right? Once a referral source has given you the name of a person to call, it's up to you to do the rest. A referral is better than a cold call because you have the name of the prospect and, if you're fortunate, you can use the name of the referral source to open the door. What more could you hope for?

Actually, there's quite a bit more you can expect from referrals that have been properly developed by their sources.

Referrals come in many different grades. We've identified ten levels of referrals that vary in quality according to how much involvement your referral source has invested in preparing the referral for you. The more time and effort your source puts into qualifying, educating, and encouraging the prospect before you become involved, the higher the quality and level of that referral. Conversely, if your referral source only passes a prospect's name to you, most of the work of converting that prospect into a customer falls on you, and the likelihood of a successful conversion diminishes significantly.

Of course, the effectiveness of your referral network in providing you with quality referrals depends on the amount of work you do to develop your sources. There are many ways to encourage them to become active and enthusiastic members of your marketing team. In this chapter, we address several methods for building the effectiveness of your referral network. The Networking Scorecard (explained in the next chapter) will enable you to track the work you are doing to develop your network. By using this scorecard to keep a weekly record of your network development efforts and the quality of referrals you receive, you'll begin to see the relationship between the two.

Now let's cover the ten levels of referrals, ranging from nothing but a name to the full Monty. We've ranked them in order of ascending quality.

1. *Name and contact information only.* This isn't much better than having just a name to call. It only indicates that your referral source has done just enough work to provide you with a phone number, address, or some other way of contacting the prospect.

2. *Literature, biography, and company information.* When a referral source offers to give a contact your marketing literature or other information about your business, all you can be certain of is that the prospect will see the materials. The prospect's interest in your product or service will depend solely on the impact of your marketing message.

3. *Authorization to use name.* Once a referral source has authorized you to use her name, you can feel fairly certain that you've established a good level of credibility with her. By allowing you to say that she endorses your product or service, your source has given you valuable leverage with the prospect; however, the problem with this level of referral is that the burden of developing the prospect still rests on you. Once you've conveyed that your referral source recommends you and your business, the task of selling really begins.

4. *General testimonial or letter of recommendation.* Getting a referral source to say or write nice things about you is a major accomplishment. His willingness to communicate positively about you and your business shows that you've built a moderate level of trust with him. Of course, testimonials and letters of recommendation are fairly common in the business world, so their impact on the average person is limited.

5. *Letter of introduction and promotion.* This is the first level of referral that truly involves a modicum of effort on the part of your referral source. Unlike the letter of recommendation, which requires little more than a written endorsement, the note or letter of introduction implies a more substantive relationship between you and the referral source, and it usually includes background information and a description of your product or service as filtered through the lens of the author. It also infers that the prospect will be hearing from you.

Adding the element of promotion increases the effectiveness of your referral source's effort on your behalf. Promotion is advocacy—an outright recommendation of your product or service with a description of its features and benefits.

6. *Introductory call and promotion.* Another level up in terms of effort is the referral source who makes a personal phone call on your behalf. It takes preparation and effort, but a telephone call from your source is more effective than a letter for paving your way to communicate with the prospect. Including a promotion makes it even more favorable.

7. *Arranged a meeting.* When your referral source arranges a meeting, she moves beyond the role of a promoter to that of a facilitator, taking the responsibility of working out the details of getting you and the prospect together. This is a big-time referral effort.

8. *In-person introduction and promotion.* At this level, your referral source is making a serious commitment of time and energy in support of your business. By agreeing to serve as an intermediary in a face-to-face introduction, your source becomes an active business agent. This demonstration of deep trust in and approval of your product or service substantially raises the referral's effectiveness with the prospect. Adding promotion further enhances its power, because your source is then actively engaged in selling your product or service instead of just facilitating a meeting.

9. *Assessment of need and interest.* In this level, your referral source has done the work of assessing the need a prospect may have for your product or service and has gauged the prospect's interest in learning more about it. This enables you to focus your selling effort on needs you know the prospect has an intention to fill, and it allows you to select or tailor your products or services to provide specific benefits.

10. *Closed deal.* At the top level, the sale has been closed before you even contact the prospect, solely on the strength of your referral source's efforts. Nothing else is required from you except to deliver the product or service and collect payment.

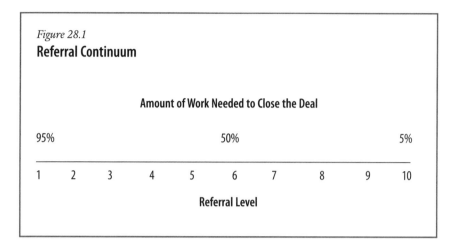

Figure 28.1
Referral Continuum

Amount of Work Needed to Close the Deal

95%					50%				5%
1	2	3	4	5	6	7	8	9	10

Referral Level

Figure 28.1 contains a continuum that shows the amount of work you have to do to close a deal, based on the level of the referral. If you're given a level 1 referral, you have to do 95 percent of the work to close; this is not much better than a cold call. On the other hand, if you get a level 9 or 10 referral, then the person giving you the referral has already done most of the work for you. It's easier for your referral source to close the deal than it is for you, because your source already has a relationship of trust with your prospect. For this reason, it's important for you to do a superb job in fulfilling that referral so your referrer will get great feedback and want to refer you again. The referral giver is, in essence, lending you her credibility; this is not something to be taken lightly.

Now that we've covered the ten levels of referrals, let's proceed to the next chapter to look at the Networking Scorecard and see how you can track the work you are doing to develop your network. (A sample Networking Scorecard can also be found in Appendix II, "Networking Like a Pro Game Plan.")

29

The Networking Scorecard

I t's a curious fact of human nature that many of us pay more attention to keeping track of our success at recreational activities than we do to tracking our success at the fundamentals of building our business. Avid golfers can tell you their handicap and recount almost shot for shot the last round they played. Bridge enthusiasts can talk for hours on strategy and exciting evenings at the card table. But how many of us who have a passion for a sport or hobby can give a detailed account of the things we did last week to strengthen our referral network?

The Networking Scorecard is a tool for keeping track of the things you do in the course of your week to build the effectiveness of your referral network. It lists a variety of activities that are proven strategies for enhancing relationships and assigns a point value to each one. Using the scorecard will both remind you to do the things listed on it and provide you with a valuable record of your networking activities and the results you can associate with them.

Sales managers around the world have continually looked for ways to measure the networking efforts of their sales forces. They want to go out and sell by networking, but most have failed to find measures of productivity they can feel confident using. The Networking Scorecard measures sales force activity in a number of ways; if the actions listed are accomplished and recorded, they can know that results will follow.

There are a number of things you can do to strengthen your relationships with your referral sources; the following tactics will build goodwill and credibility. Of course, this is not an exhaustive list, so feel free to add your own actions to it.

SEND A THANK-YOU CARD

Always a nice gesture, a handwritten thank-you card makes a great impression, especially in this age of electronic communication. Be sure to write a personalized note that mentions what you're thanking your referral source for. As we said before, SendOut Cards.com is a great resource for this.

SEND A GIFT

A gift is always welcome. Like a thank-you card, a gift, however small or inexpensive, builds visibility and credibility with your referral source. Try to find out what your referral source likes (favorite foods, hobbies, or other things) and send a gift that is personalized to her tastes.

CALL A REFERRAL SOURCE

An occasional phone call is a good way to keep the relationship strong, if you take care to call only when it's least likely to be an unwelcome interruption. It's also a good idea to have a piece of news or some tidbit of information to pass along that will benefit or interest your source.

ARRANGE A ONE-TO-ONE MEETING

Meeting a referral source in person is an excellent opportunity to learn more about his business and interests. Prepare some questions in advance so that the conversation flows smoothly. Be ready to give an update on your business and to ask lots of questions about your source's interests.

EXTEND AN INVITATION

Invite a referral source to a networking event. Introducing her to other businesspeople you know gives your source an opportunity to meet others in your target market and may also provide new business opportunities.

SET UP AN ACTIVITY

A recreational activity, such as a golf outing, fishing trip, concert, or play, is a great opportunity to let your referral source see a different side of you in an informal setting. The activity should be one that will give everybody time to relax, but it may also include an element of information such as a speech or educational presentation. To maximize the effectiveness of your time with your sources, you should invite no more than four people and spend at least one hour with each.

OFFER A REFERRAL

Giving your referral source a referral is a wonderful way to build your relationship. By helping build your source's business, you create a debt of gratitude that will encourage your source to respond in kind.

SEND AN ARTICLE OF INTEREST

Set up a file for holding newspaper and magazine clippings that may be of interest to people you would like to be your referral sources. Sending an article, especially one that is pertinent to your source's current business or personal circumstances, says you are thinking about your source's needs.

ARRANGE A GROUP ACTIVITY FOR CLIENTS

Gathering your clients together creates an excellent environment for synergy and for raising your credibility with all. The one thing the people in this group will definitely have in common is you, so you'll certainly be the focus of a good many conversations. Group activities may be social, such as a barbecue or a ball game, or they may be educational, such as a seminar or a demonstration.

NOMINATE A REFERRAL SOURCE

Watch for opportunities to nominate a referral source for an award. Local service and civic organizations often present annual awards recognizing contributions to a particular cause, and local periodicals often sponsor awards contests for businesspeople. Find out what groups and interests your referral source is involved in, and check to see if there is any form of recognition associated with them.

DISPLAY A SOURCE'S BROCHURE

Doing a bit of sales work on behalf of a referral source can only enhance your relationship. If you have a public area for your business, offer to place your source's materials where your clients can read them.

INCLUDE A SOURCE IN YOUR NEWSLETTER

Even a brief mention of a referral source in your newsletter can pay dividends down the road, including the opportunity for your source to reciprocate with his newsletter.

ARRANGE A SPEAKING ENGAGEMENT

Help your referral source get in front of a group that would be interested in her business or area of expertise. Local chapters of service organizations, such as Rotary and Kiwanis, are always looking for good speakers. If you belong to a group that invites people to speak, use your contacts to help your source make the rounds among various chapters.

INVITE A SOURCE TO JOIN YOUR ADVISORY BOARD

Set up an informal board of advisors with whom you can meet regularly. Ask a referral source who you feel could contribute valuable insights to sit on your board. You can communicate with your board members via phone, e-mail, newsletter, or occasional group meetings. Having an advisory board is important because people generally work best when they are accountable to someone other than themselves for accomplishing certain tasks. It's too easy to procrastinate when we have no one to answer to but ourselves. Whether you're starting a diet, beginning an exercise routine, or growing and developing your referral network, involving another person or group of people in the process will greatly enhance your chances for success.

Here's a riddle that illustrates the point of accountability: Five frogs sat on a log at the edge of a pond. Four of the frogs decided

Figure 29.1

Networking Scorecard Worksheet

Week of:								
Action	**Points**	**Mon**	**Tue**	**Wed**	**Thur**	**Fri**	**Total**	
Send a thank-you card	1×							
Send a gift	1×							
Call someone in your network	1×							
Arrange a one-to-one	5×							
Attend a networking event (bring someone +5)	5×							
Set up an activity—max 4 people, 1 hour/person	10×							
Offer a referral (level = points; 16 shades)								
Send an article of interest	5×							
Arrange a group activity for clients	50×							
Nominate someone	10×							
Display another's brochures (first time only)	5×							
Include others in newsletter	5×							
Arrange a speaking engagement	10×							
Set up an advisory board (per person)	10×							
Write and sign an agreement (level 3)	10×							
One thing that would help your business								
Another thing that would help your business								
Total								

Figure 29.1

Networking Scorecard Worksheet, continued

Business by Referral Score

Less than 30 points	=	Some
30–50 points	=	Fair
50–75 points	=	Good/consistent
75–100 points	=	Excellent
100 or more	=	Fantastic/You are or will soon be doing 100% of your business by referral.

©Referral Institute 2007

to jump into the pond. How many frogs were left sitting on the log? Answer: Five. Deciding to jump in and actually jumping are two different things.

Deciding to do the work of developing your network's effectiveness is only the first step in the process. You have to *do* it. The Networking Scorecard (Figure 29.1) is an excellent tool for holding yourself accountable for consistently doing the work that will enhance your network.

Credibility-Enhancing Materials Checklist

Below is a checklist of items you may already have available or wish to begin assembling, which can be used as collateral materials in developing your desired image. Be sure to store such materials efficiently by purchasing a bin or a set of shelves built to make it easy to retrieve frequently used documents. Such units usually come with cubbyholes that are 3 or 4 across and 12, 18, or 24 down. This equipment greatly aids any company's word-of-mouth campaign and ability to respond quickly when necessary.

CHECKLIST OF MATERIALS FOR DEVELOPING YOUR WORD-OF-MOUTH CAMPAIGN

- ❏ Testimonial letters from satisfied clients
- ❏ Photos of yourself and your office facilities, equipment, and products
- ❏ Photos of your key customers
- ❏ Photos of awards and certificates you and your staff have earned
- ❏ Articles in which you're mentioned
- ❏ Articles you have published
- ❏ A one-page, *faxable* flier
- ❏ Unpublished articles
- ❏ Audio or videos you have used
- ❏ Any of your new-product announcements or press releases that have been published
- ❏ Copies of other display advertisements that you've used (text from radio or TV spots)
- ❏ Advertisements that you've run
- ❏ A list of your memberships and affiliations
- ❏ Product catalogs you use
- ❏ Current brochures, circulars, and data sheets
- ❏ Question-and-answer sheets
- ❏ Logos, trademarks, service marks, patterns, designs you've used
- ❏ Your letterhead and stationery
- ❏ Your annual report, capability statement, and prospectus
- ❏ Newsletters or news-type publications you use
- ❏ Your motto, mission statement, or service pledge
- ❏ Client or customer proposals and bid sheets
- ❏ Survey results by you or others
- ❏ Presentation notes or slides and PowerPoint presentations
- ❏ Marketing letters you wrote to clients

CHECKLIST OF MATERIALS FOR DEVELOPING YOUR WORD-OF-MOUTH CAMPAIGN, CONTINUED

❑ Generic materials developed by your associations

❑ Articles on trends affecting your target market

❑ Posters, banners, and display materials used at trade shows

Note: This is not a complete list of items needed to market your business. The items in this list are focused on enhancing your networking activities.

Networking Like a Pro Game Plan

**YOUR PLAYBOOK WITH THE SECRET PLAN FOR
NETWORKING LIKE A PRO**

FIRST QUARTER (FIRST 30 DAYS)

Begin by understanding and using the tremendous power of your database. A great database tool we use is Relate2Profit.com. Use the coupon code "NLP" for 30 days free and 50% off.

Play 1: Identify your profitable players using the VCP Process®.

List top 20 in Visibility (see Chapter 17).

	Name	Company	Contact Info
1.			
2.			
3.			
4.			
5.			
6.			
7.			
8.			
9.			
10.			
11.			
12.			
13.			
14.			
15.			
16.			
17.			
18.			
19.			
20.			

List top 20 in Credibility.

	Name	Company	Contact Info
1.			
2.			
3.			
4.			
5.			
6.			
7.			
8.			
9.			
10.			
11.			
12.			
13.			
14.			
15.			
16.			
17.			
18.			
19.			
20.			

List top 10 in Profitability.

	Name	Company	Contact Info
1.			
2.			
3.			
4.			
5.			
6.			
7.			
8.			
9.			
10.			

Remember to activate your network using the Networking Scorecard. Do this every week. Important note: Do this with someone else; have an accountability partner.

Play 2: Get connected in the community.

Pick three of the following organizations and join them. Remember to get involved and definitely join a strong-contact organization

Network Type	Date to Visit	Joined On
Strong contact (BNI)		
Casual contact (Chamber)		
Civic or service club		
Religious		
Online		
Knowledge or trade		
Social		
Women's business associations		
Other		

Play 3: Givers Gain.

Remember to apply the law of reciprocity.

Meet five people you have a visible relationship with and determine what you can do to move the relationship to Credible.

Person	Meeting Location and Date	Action Steps Taken
1.		
2.		
3.		
4.		
5.		

Meet five people you have a credible relationship with and determine what you can do to move the relationship to Profitable

Person	Meeting Location and Date	Action Steps Taken
1.		
2.		
3.		
4.		
5.		

SECOND QUARTER

Target market is important, and being specific about it makes you easy to refer to.

Play 1: Identify your target market.

List three people or businesses most likely to use your products and services.

1. _____

2. _____

3. _____

List three people or businesses that can refer you to the people above. These are your referral sources.

1. _____

2. _____

3. _____

Play 2: Determine the ultimate benefit of your product.

List 10 benefits. (Hint: not your product or service)

1. _____

2. _____

3. _____

4. _____

5. _____

6. _____

7. _____

8. _____

9. _____

10. _____

Which is the biggest benefit, and which one resonates with your target market?

Idea: Survey your current clients to discover this. What are people really buying from you?

Play 3: Create your very own USP (unique selling proposition).

This will be used to make your message specific to prospects, referral sources, and others in your network.

Here are a few examples:

- "I help busy entrepreneurs market their business in less than 90 days."—Brian Hilliard, sales and marketing coach
- "I help nonprofit organizations connect with their community through the game of golf."—John Parker, golf fundraising specialist
- "I help people network like a pro by teaching them highly effective referral systems."—David Alexander, Chief Networking Officer, Referrals 4 Life
- "I work with municipalities on capital improvement projects in the areas of water, wastewater, and drainage."—Sharmaine James, project engineer in New Orleans

Now write three for yourself and pick the one you like best.

1. _____

2. _____

3. _____

THIRD QUARTER

Be the best player you can be.

> "Winning is not a sometime thing; it's an all-the-time thing. You don't win once
> in a while, you don't do things right once in a while, you do them right all the
> time. Winning is a habit; unfortunately, losing is too." —Vince Lombardi

Play 1: Quality, not quantity.

Limit yourself to five to ten new contacts per event. Look for groups of people who are open to
your approach. Many people make the mistake of casting their nets too wide. We recommend
going only to events where you can be personally introduced to others.

Here are a few things to remember when it comes to meeting new people:

- You're not interested in selling anything to the person you're just meeting; you want to
  find some way you can help her. You understand, of course, that what goes around
  comes around, usually in the form of referrals for your business.
- You want to create a visible identity with everyone you meet. A visible identity is the
  answer to this question: "How can I differentiate myself, in the mind of this other person,
  from the other five people she's already met?"

List five events you will attend, the people you will invite to go with you, and people you would
like to be introduced to at each event.

	Event	Who's Going wih You	When	Whom You Need to Meet
1.				
2.				
3.				
4.				
5.				

Remember to spend five to seven minutes talking *and mostly listening* to each person you meet.

Then follow up with your new contacts to further your initial discussions.

Person	Follow-Up	Follow-Up Activity	When

Play 2: Culitivate win-win referral relationships.

Remember this diagram:

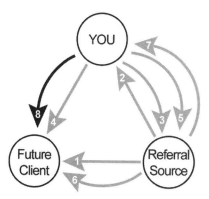

Who should win in any referral relationship? Everyone. That way, more referrals will come your way.

List the last 10 referrals you received, who gave them, and actions you took to make the referral source look like a hero.

1. _____
   _____

2. _____
   _____

3. _____
   _____

4. _____
   _____

5. _____
   _____

6. _____
   _____

7. _____
   _____

8. _____
   _____

9. _____
   _____

10. _____
    _____

FOURTH QUARTER

Use the Networking Scorecard to accelerate and track your success. Keeping score improves the score. Use the following spreadsheet to start tracking your referrals.

The Pro Networker's Referral Tracking System

Date	Referral's Name	Referred By	Contacted Referral On (date)	Interest —Hot —Warm —Tepid —Cold	Meet On (date)	Follow-Up Meeting(s) On Date(s)	Status —Closed (Sold) —Might Close —No Close	Approximate Value (if closed)	Spin-Offs —Yes (How Many) —No

Play 1: Set your referral goals.

1. How much in pocket money do you wish to make over the next 12 months?

2. How much money do you make per transaction, on average?

3. What is your closing percentage?

4. How many referrals will you need over the next 12 months to achieve your goal?

_____

_____

5. How many referral sources do you need to achieve this?

_____

_____

Play 2: Use your scorecard.

Do this and tally the score each week. This alone will have a massive impact on your networking success.

Week of:

Action	Points	Mon	Tue	Wed	Thur	Fri	Total
Send a thank-you card	1×						
Send a gift	1×						
Call someone in your network	1×						
Arrange a one-to-one	5×						
Attend a networking event (bring someone +5)	5×						
Set up an activity—max 4 people, 1 hour/person	10×						
Offer a referral (level = points; 16 shades)							
Send an article of interest	5×						
Arrange a group activity for clients	50×						
Nominate someone	10×						
Display another's brochures (first time only)	5×						
Include others in newsletter	5×						

Action	Points	Mon	Tue	Wed	Thur	Fri	Total
Arrange a speaking engagement	10×						
Set up an advisory board (per person)	10×						
Write and sign an agreement (level 3)	10×						
One thing that would help your business							
Another thing that would help your business							
Total							

Business by Referral Score

Less than 30 points	=	Some
30–50 points	=	Fair
50–75 points	=	Good/consistent
75–100 points	=	Excellent
100 or more	=	Fantastic/You are or will soon be doing 100% of your business by referral.

©Referral Institute 2007

Play 3: Become a hub.

A hub firm is the key business in a constellation of businesses tethered to one another to make the most of each firm's products, services, or expertise. List the types of firms that you should build partnerships or alliances with to better enable you to serve your market. These include businesses that fall within your contact sphere; however, they may include other businesses, such as competitors with different specialties. Once you've listed these companies, set appointments with each to begin the relationship-building process. See if there are any joint venture projects that you can conduct with them on a trial basis.

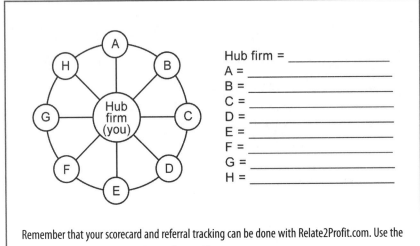

Hub firm = _____

A = _____

B = _____

C = _____

D = _____

E = _____

F = _____

G = _____

H = _____

Remember that your scorecard and referral tracking can be done with Relate2Profit.com. Use the coupon code "NLP" for 30 days free and 50% off.

POSTGAME PRESS CONFERENCE
Referral Rewards Programs

List three different rewards programs you can use to thank your referral sources.

1. _____

2. _____

3. _____

Idea: If you really want to take it to the next level, create a separate referral rewards program for each of your sources. Remember, your reward should not be what you want to give; it should be what your source wants to receive.

Extend your reach.

Who is willing to actively promote you to clients? List at least five people in your network and an action each one can take to promote your business.

	Person	Action	Date to Ask	Date Person Will Do It
1.				
2.				
3.				
4.				
5.				

Rate Your Efforts

1 = Never 3 = Sometimes 5 = Always

I have a referral plan and work the plan.	1 2 3 4 5
I track where all of my referrals come from.	1 2 3 4 5
I have a firm understanding of my target market.	1 2 3 4 5
I know the amount of business that I generate by referral.	1 2 3 4 5
I have a thank-you system for all of my referral sources.	1 2 3 4 5
I have an organized database system that is easy to use.	1 2 3 4 5
I keep my database updated regularly.	1 2 3 4 5
I have a mission statement for myself and my company.	1 2 3 4 5
I understand how to develop a referral partner.	1 2 3 4 5
I know the value of an appointment.	1 2 3 4 5
I have written goals for all of my networking groups.	1 2 3 4 5
I have a systematic approach for motivating my referral sources.	1 2 3 4 5
I have a system for staying in contact with my referral sources.	1 2 3 4 5
I know how many referrals I need to keep my pipeline full.	1 2 3 4 5
I know how to do focused networking.	1 2 3 4 5
I have a clear benefit statement for each of my products.	1 2 3 4 5
I understand the benefits of my products or services.	1 2 3 4 5
I have the ability to implement a new system in my business.	1 2 3 4 5
I understand the value of coaching and accountability partners.	1 2 3 4 5
I consistently get high-level referrals from my referral sources.	1 2 3 4 5
Total	

100	Networking like pro
80–99	A little tweaking needed
60–79	This is the IF System at work
40–59	Leads appear, but quite by accident
20–39	Lots of work needed, but it is a place to start

About the Authors

Dr. Ivan Misner is the Founder and Chairman of BNI, the world's largest business networking organization. BNI was founded in 1985. The organization now has over thousands of groups throughout every populated continent of the world. Each year, BNI, generates  millions of referrals resulting in billions of dollars worth of business for its members.

Ivan's Ph.D. is from the University of Southern California. He has written 11 books, including his *New York Times* bestseller

Masters of Networking as well as his recent number-one bestseller, *The 29% Solution*. He is a monthly columnist for Entrepreneur.com and is the Senior Partner for the Referral Institute, a referral training company with trainers around the world. In addition, he has taught business management and social capital courses at several universities throughout the United States.

Called the Father of Modern Networking by CNN and the Networking Guru by *Entrepreneur* magazine, Ivan is considered to be one of the world's leading experts on business networking and has been a keynote speaker for major corporations and associations throughout the world. He has been featured in the *Los Angeles Times, Wall Street Journal,* and *New York Times,* as well as numerous TV and radio shows on CNN, CNBC, and the BBC in London.

Ivan is on the Board of Trustees for the University of LaVerne. He is also the Founder of the BNI-Misner Charitable Foundation and was recently named Humanitarian of the Year by a southern California newspaper. He is married and lives with his wife, Elisabeth, and their three children in Claremont, California. *In his spare time(!!!),* he is also an amateur magician and a black belt in karate.

David Alexander has a vision is to build a thriving community of professionals who believe that investing in others' success is the path to prosperity. David creates this vision through being the CNO (Chief Networking Officer) of Referrals4life LLC.

Referrals4life operates BNI franchises in North Carolina, Louisiana, Georgia, and Mississippi. David's company is also part of the world's leading referral training organization, the Referral Institute.

David is a respected author and keynote presenter. His books convey his passion and mission of teaching people how to create success, with a strong emphasis on referral marketing. David is blessed to be living the life of his dreams and wants others to have the same opportunity. His most recent book is *Roadmap to Success,* written with Stephen Covey and Ken Blanchard. He is also working on three other books, *GPS for Success, Referrals for Life,* and *Fire Up Your Referrals.*

David and his team have won numerous awards with BNI and the Referral Institute, including BNI Hall of Fame, Top Ten Region, Excellence in Goal Setting Analysis and Planning, Top Directors Performance Reviews, Most New Members During Member Extravaganza, and Top Producer. David is also a member of BNI's Founders Circle and Platinum Club.

David graduated from Western Carolina University, where he was an active member of the Lambda Chi Alpha fraternity. He currently resides with the love of his life, Kimberly, and their two children, Christian and Peyton, in Marietta, Georgia. He is very fortunate to be very involved with his family; if school is out, so is David. He enjoys running, working out, skiing, hiking, camping, and spending quality time with family and friends.

David has taught thousands of businesspeople and companies how to network like a pro, teaching them to dramatically increase their business referrals. David can show your company how to increase sales by 30 percent, 50 percent, or even 100 percent through enhancing relationships you already have and creating new ones. David is a firm believer in Givers Gain and is driven to help others achieve success.

Brian Hilliard, a popular speaker and creator of the program How to Market Your Business in Less Than 90 Days, is considered one of the leading authorities in showing busy entrepreneurs how to get more business right away.

Some of Brian's work has appeared nationally in *Black Enterprise* magazine, at About.com, and on the *Martha Zoller Morning Show,* where his interview was broadcast to over two million listeners.

Brian has also produced a CD, *How to Talk So Your Prospects Will Listen,* and he's best known for delivering dynamic, thought-provoking workshops that keep people coming back. As an avid reader in management, economics, and communication, Brian brings a unique perspective to all of his clients.

Some of Brian's clients include Kraft Foods, National Financial Services Group, and the American Express Small Business Expo.

The Referral Institute is a leading referral training organization, with franchises, trainers, and coaches around the  world. The organization teaches business professionals how to harness the power of referral marketing to drive sales for long-term, sustainable business growth by referral. Founded in 2001, the Referral Institute began developing training materials specific to referral marketing and was recently recognized by Entrepreneur.com as one of the top 500 franchised companies in the world.

The Referral Institute's mission is to help people create Referrals for Life®. In total, the Referral Institute provides the world's leading material on referral marketing.

The organization offers students one-day programs as well as courses covering several modules over 10 to 12 weeks. The Pipeline Program, the organization's signature class, requires participants to attend the class with a referral source. The one-day Pipeline Seminar teaches a simple, highly manageable referral process by which participants leave the training having already scheduled appointments with qualified prospects.

The Referral Institute's 10- to 12-week course is called Certified Networker®. This course is truly a foundation for understanding, developing, and tracking your referral business. In most cases, Certified Networker simply changes the way business owners do business. It narrows their target market, provides them with mission statements, and shows them how profitable it can be to develop referral sources by being strategic. Certified Networker is a must for anyone new to referral marketing.

Please go to referralinstitute.com to learn more about referral marketing as well as how to attend a Referral Institute training program in your area. You may contact the organization at info@referralinstitute.com to talk about growing your business by generating qualified referrals.

BNI, the world's largest business networking organization, was founded by Dr. Ivan Misner in 1985 as a way for businesspeople to generate referrals in a structured,  professional environment. The organization, now the world's largest referral business network, has thousands of chapters with tens of thousands of members on every populated continent. Since the orgaization's inception, BNI members have passed millions of referrals, generating billions of dollars in business for the participants.

The primary purpose of the organization is to pass qualified business referrals to its members. The philosophy of BNI can be summed up in two simple words: Givers Gain®. If you give business to people, you will get business from them. BNI allows only one person per profession to join a chapter. The program is designed to help businesspeople develop long-term relationships, thereby creating a basis for trust and, inevitably, referrals. The mission of BNI is to help members increase their business through a structured, positive, and professional word-of-mouth program that enables them to develop long-term, meaningful relationships with quality business professionals.

To visit a chapter near you, contact BNI via e-mail at bni@bni.com or visit its website at bni.com.

Index